MW00856777

Letters From The Other Side

Letters From The Other Side

With Love, Harry and Helen

written down
by Mary
Blount White.

UPPER ACCESS PUBLISHERS
HINESBURG, VERMONT
1987

Upper Access Publishers
One Upper Access Road
P.O. Box 457
Hinesburg, Vermont 05461
802-482-2988

Cover art and illuminations by Ella Lynn Brackett

Library of Congress Cataloguing in Publication Data

Blount, Harry, 1880-1913 (Spirit)
  Letters from the other side.

  1. Spirit writings. 2. Future life. 3. Reincarnation. I. Blount, Helen, 1876-1892 (Spirit) II. White, Mary Blount, 1866-1947. III. Title.
BF1301.B52   1987   133.9'3   87-25318

ISBN 0-942679-02-4
ISBN 0-942679-03-2 (pbk.)

10 9 8 7 6 5 4 3 2 1

TABLE OF CONTENTS   Page

Contents

Contents

Contents

Contents

A NEW INTRODUCTION:
WHY THESE LETTERS ARE BEING PUBLISHED NOW

Mary Blount White was a great-aunt I never knew. But through her gift of these letters, she has had a profound effect on my life. A pamphlet of some of the letters from Harry and Helen was guarded in our house, almost as a family secret. "Don't tell other people about this," we were told. "They won't understand." Yet the letters provided the help and comfort I needed to cope with the death of my mother when I was 13. Since then, the letters have helped repeatedly to clarify my sense of meaning in life and to overcome any fear of "death."

To this day, I find new insights every time I reread the letters. They hold so much that one reading is not enough. The messages from Harry and Helen are timeless, as true and as relevant today as they were in 1917. There seems little that might offend or contradict anyone's personal religious beliefs. Although the letters are for specific family members, the larger messages, with their emphasis on love, can provide guidance to all persons of good will.

Mary White's mother, Lucia Blount, recognized the universality of the messages and made clear her desire to share them with the rest of humanity. The introduction she wrote in 1917 and her footnotes are included in this volume. At her urging, Harry and Helen, through their sister, agreed to allow their letters to be published, but circulation of the letters was limited at that time.

In recent years, there has been a great interest in channelled information from the spirit world. I personally find that an encouraging hopeful development. It seems the right time to make these letters

7

available to the general public.

In preparation for this printing, Mary's son, John Sargent White, has described in eloquent terms the reasons for agreeing to share the letters with a larger audience:

> (The letters) were personal messages from a devoted brother and sister who had died. They were not intended for public distribution. My grandmother, however, thought that they should be disclosed because they could do much good.
>
> During World War I young soldiers who were invited to "the Oaks"[1] for Sunday dinner read a small pamphlet containing a selection of the letters and were greatly heartened. One said, "Now I'm not afraid to die!" The letters show that there is more to the after-life than playing a harp and singing hymns through all eternity.
>
> The point is that personality does not change after death. One can't enjoy the creature comforts, but humor, fellowship, character, and love carry over the divide. That takes away the fear of the unknown.

In reading the letters, one caution should be observed from the outset. Without a conscious memory of any previous existence in the spirit world, some of us tend to embrace as fact, without question, that which is presented as spiritual guidance, *even when the spirit source warns against such blind acceptance.* Harry makes the same guarded statements here.

An analogy may be useful. If you were planning your first trip to China, for example, you might want to read accounts by people who have already been there. But there are many such accounts and they are all different because each traveler to China

---

[1]*Lucia Blount's home was Dumbarton Oaks, now a museum in Washington, DC.*

encounters different adventures. A doctor, a businessperson, a steelworker, and an archeologist may each notice different things. But if you have read a great many accounts by those people who have been to China, you will have a better perspective on what life is actually like there, and you will be better prepared for your own visit.

There are fewer reports from travelers to the other side, and proof is hard to establish. Harry felt moved in an early letter to prove his identity by having Mary replicate his signature *(letter number 5 in this printing)*.

Today's readers, outside the family, don't have the benefit of that proof. That may explain, in part, Mary's reluctance to share her gift with others. Sargent White comments:

> Mother had a great gift and never used it for personal gain. The idea of being a public medium was repugnant to her. The gift should not be wasted to satisfy idle curiosity.
>
> Many of the later letters were never written down. Dad would ask a question and Mother's finger would move on her knee to spell out the answer. For example:
>
> "How do you like the new barn I built?"
>
> "Bully! Keep up the good work!"
>
> More serious questions, requiring long answers, required the use of pencil and yellow pad.

The only real "proof" of the legitimacy of these letters is in the reading. The loving, caring messages could only have come from spirits whose motivation was to help. Harry and Helen consider themselves students, who are willing to pass along their observations to us, but who feel they still have much to learn. They even admit to mistakes, correcting misinformation from earlier letters in later ones. On complex subjects such as reincarnation, early letters are vague and doubtful, while subsequent letters provide rich detail.

They also acknowledge the limitations of language, which contains no words to explain concepts that exist outside this plane. Therefore, they resort to analogies, which may not be entirely accurate, but which nevertheless may provide insights into issues that we cannot fully understand.

This book has prompted me to become an avid reader of a variety of spiritual material. The words of Harry and Helen are not inconsistent with those of other spirits and channelers who have become well known. Seth, Jason, Edgar Cayce, and others have given us information about the plane where Harry and Helen exist, but from different perspectives. At least for me, reading of other spiritual insights has complemented, rather than contradicted, the insights in this book.

The letters would have crumbled with other pages of forgotten history were it not for the special encouragement of two people. One is the man who introduced the letters to me at an early age: my father, Dr. E. Rodman Shippen. During preparation of this book he wrote the following reminiscence:

> Mary Blount White, my mother's sister, never liked the sound of "Aunt Mary," so we always called her "Tante." Although she had been blinded by scarlet fever in childhood, she was never bitter; she was always very loving and had a delicious sense of humor. Tante's husband, Uncle Thurlow (Tee in the book) was quiet but very understanding, kind and considerate.
>
> When my mother explained reincarnation to me, it made very good sense. And then when I read the Harry and Helen letters everything fell into place. I shall always treasure Tante's two-word philosophy of life: LOVE, SERVE.

The other person who made this book possible is Sargent White. He is Mrs. White's only child, referred to often in the book as "John." He has earned great respect and admiration as a prominent scientist and engineer. His decision to allow publication of these personal family letters required great courage, and there will be many who are grateful for his sharing.

ELIZABETH BLOUNT SHIPPEN

PREFATORY NOTE, 1917

I have been asked to tell how I first came to know I could write automatically. It was soon after my sister's death when my mother's thoughts were turned to the possibility or probability of conscious existence after death, and she was seeking light on the subject, that I heard, for the first time, about the Ouija Board, and secured one out of curiosity. The results were rather startling, and interested us both. I found that I had more power to move the pointer than anyone in the house.

We received messages from Helen, and none of the nonsensical stuff often called out by the ordinary users of the board, who ask foolish questions and make a game of it. It was a serious matter to my mother. Finally, after several weeks of occasional sittings, and spelling out of messages, it suddenly occurred to me one evening that I had heard of people getting messages through the hand and I became eager to see what I could do. I asked Papa for a pencil and the moment it touched the paper I felt as if I held a galvanic battery in my hand.

After a few written words I felt my arm quiver from the shoulder down and I said, "Why I could write a lot," and securing a pad, wrote many pages, getting a letter from a brother of my mother who had met Helen, and explained to her that she had died, and was not having a bad dream, as she had supposed. He said that a feeling of bitterness toward my father had held him back, and that when he had taken Helen on his knee, and dried her tears of distress, and explained to her about her present state, the hard spot had melted from his heart, and he was able to "go on." He said that he had not

12

known whose child it was he had been sent to help until he had her in his arms.

All this talk was Greek to me. I scarcely knew this Uncle who died when I was small, and I had never heard of "going on"; in fact a more ignorant person than I was on such topics could hardly have been found. I was not only ignorant but indifferent.

To please my mother, who seemed greatly comforted by letters from Helen, I continued to write automatically upon various occasions for about three years. I had a mild curiosity but no deep feeling and no personal pleasure, and finally was greatly bored by friends begging me to try to get some messages from their lost relatives. I hated the idea of being called a "medium" and, the keenness of my mother's grief having become softened by time and lightened by these letters, I abandoned the writing altogether, and for more than twenty years had received nothing although I had sat once or twice during that time with no results. Consequently, believing I had lost my former power, it was rather startling to feel the old quiver along my arm again and the impulse to sit for Helen.

In the later years Helen had been almost daily in my thoughts, though I never expected to hear from her again. I was sitting alone one day in the practice room of a private conservatory of music in New York City, waiting for an aunt who was late for her appointment; and feeling the impulse so strongly to write, I went next door, and borrowed paper and pencil; then, instead of Helen's free message, came a cramped, hesitating scrawl from Harry, chiding me for not writing for him, as I had for Helen.

This was the beginning of the second flood of letters from the other side. This time I was delighted to receive them, and most grateful for their coming. One's heart and brain expand after twenty-three years.

MARY BLOUNT WHITE

13

INTRODUCTION, 1917

In presenting these letters to the public I feel that a little explanation is demanded.

In 1892 my 16-year-old daughter Mary, discovering she could write automatically, received what we considered remarkable messages from one so young. A prominent clergyman, who has himself written much upon life after death, considered them worth publishing, and offered to edit them; but we shrank from publicity, so that only our intimate friends shared them with us.

Then, after more than twenty years of silence, came these letters from Harry and Helen, and the contents seemed to us so remarkable that in December, 1914, we had printed a small pamphlet containing a few of the letters, which we sent to relatives and friends as a Christmas gift. This pamphlet, being read by others, brought such an avalanche of letters, asking for copies, begging for another edition, and telling us we could not realize how eager the world was for just such messages as these letters contained, that we felt we could no longer refuse to give the letters to the world.

It was a very difficult matter to decide what to omit in such a mass of very personal letters; especially as we felt we ought to put in every thing which in our opinion might be helpful to other troubled or struggling souls. Even though all these ideas of love and self-sacrifice are to be found in the Bible, yet it does help sometimes to have specifications.

I know I have worked harder to down the "old Adam" in me than ever before; and several of my friends claim that the few letters in the pamphlet have caused them to face about and look at life

14

differently. To me the book will be of no value unless it can do just that.

The reader will notice the very distinct personality of each writer, and will observe how Harry progresses. In life, while he was a firm believer in reincarnation, he seldom went to church, and he would never allow me to talk on these matters or to read "spirit messages" to him, because he said he was not at all afraid to die, and that we could never know in this life about these things; it was guesswork with every one, and he was satisfied to know when he arrived on the other side.

I respected his feelings, but "Sister" insisted on talking with him that last summer, while we were all at the seashore. He thanked her for that in one of the first letters.

I put in a letter from my mother because it was so old-fashioned and exactly as she used to speak, showing a decided difference in style; and then some of it seems to me quite touching, and that might help others. I struggled for months against the idea of exposing our tenderest feelings to outsiders. Harry's shrinking from "being made a show of" he takes straight from me. But nothing ever touches others' hearts unless it comes live and palpitating from one's own heart. So I finally came to be willing to let the world have what had seemed valuable and intimate to me.

I thought at first to make it anonymous, but many friends begged me to come out boldly with my own name, to face the world's skepticism, and that of some members of my own family too! I have yielded to their opinions.

Should these letters appeal to anyone as true, and be an inspiration to live the life of brotherhood more nearly, I shall feel it quite worth the effort it takes to share these intimate and dear messages from my own people.

LUCIA E. BLOUNT

September, 1916
The Oaks, Washington, D.C.

15

THIS IS NO HOLY PLACE . . .
SIN IS NOT WHAT YOU AND I
THOUGHT IT WAS.

November 14, 1913

ister, don't tell anyone of this writing; it is better not. I only want to be of use, and not to be made a show of; so cut out the publicity stuff and keep mum.

Shucks, this is no holy place I've struck, so why affect the part? I am well, surely, and strong as before, but don't forget I have plenty to correct in myself. It's me for my small boy these days. I sit for hours, watching him, trying to see how and where to begin his instruction. He has to acquire poise, and it's up to me, I imagine.

Papa's mind is divided, as part of it is on this side forming his new body. It's a peach too, tall and strong and sweet. This is a big world, and a bully place to be in, believe me. Sin is not what you and I thought it was, but merely animal excess in life force, spilling over, not soul-shrivelling as we dreaded. Anyway it looks so to me, but I haven't begun to get a line on how the game stacks up here yet, being, as it were, a tenderfoot. All the tales you told me, utterly against my will, surely helped out. I am glad now you were so persistent about filling me up. Don't worry about writing what I am trying to get over. You can't go far wrong, and if I see you getting beside the mark I'll quit.

HARRY

16

FORM, TONE, COLOR, SPIRIT: WORDS FAIL . . . A SUGGESTION SUFFICES FOR THE MOMENT.

2

November 21, 1913

ister, please forgive me for being so awfully blind and selfish this past summer. I can see now I was not half myself, and . . .

HARRY

Harry is too weak to write, Sister. I am here, Helen. Yes, it is years since I have written, but I have been on the upper planes working at fine things, really big things. Yes, violin, and also color. I am working on color with musical tones at high rates of vibration, which also register in form. All things have roots in common. That is the beauty of the work here, its relation not to allied arts, but to material expression of life forms. Creations have, first, life as the tap root; then form, then tone, then color, then spirit; what you call character, or temperamental essence. Oh, words fail me here. I can't now express what I mean. One needs a larger vocabulary to convey a sense of these higher forms of life. No matter, you get a suggestion of the idea, which suffices for the moment.

When artists fail, it is mainly from the lack of proper balance, due to over-stimulation of certain

17

destructive qualities springing from selfishness. Success is as easy as failure. If you and I could only see the whole structure for one illuminating instant! It is the digging out of the thing, one limb at a time, which requires such tedious effort. Two elements combine to bring this about; first the building of the individual ego as an independent force; and second, the bringing into proper relationship of this three-fold nature: atomic, mental, and psychic. No, three-fold is not as the word is used with you. The three-fold unit of life is that which registers on different planes of expression, so when an artist turns too far in one direction he finds that destiny, or law, steps in. Success is only the knowledge which belongs to Truth, and that has no fear of so called death, or change. I happen to be one of the humbler students of art, and was fortunate enough to escape here long before being taught the false standards of art and success on your plane. It is a boon for which I cannot be too grateful.

Tell my brother Tee[2] that what he most lacks is not a chance, but a more direct contact with his fellow humans. Let him get at that side of his art[3] and he will have all the work he can perform, both there and here. This art is one of the most comprehensive, and takes a high rank here as a developer of individual growth, as you may readily see. His career is being thwarted at that point, so what he must do is to sit in the silence, and wait till his inner sense tells him what is needed to right his balance, and allow his further progress; that is, if he is really a true artist, one of the elect, as it were. The sham product achieves worldly success, and

---

[2] *Helen died years before her sister Mary married "Tee," by which nickname the members of her family addressed her husband. - L.E.B.*

[3] *He was an actor. - L.E.B.*

arrives here a blank. His foundation has been laid narrowly, so his structure topples over as soon as the truth breathes upon it.

HELEN

ARRIVAL ON THE OTHER SIDE . . .   3

Thanksgiving,
November 27, 1913

ere we are, Sister. Harry wants me to write first, as he is too weak to push through the separating wall of neutral matter which lies between your plane and ours. Tell Mamma that when Harry left his body he was not at all aware he was gone until he saw me beside him instead of the doctor; and, too, he came through the dark belt in a few seconds, so was full of thoughts, and almost words he had been using there. The sight of my face startled him, and made him take himself to task for sleeping so soon after dinner. Then I laughed, and something about that giggle recalled his little boy memory of me. He smiled at me, saying: "Am I really out of it at last, and is this Helen? Sister said last summer you would be on hand when I came over here. My, but you are good to look at. I had forgotten what fine eyes you had. I remember now, and that habit of wrinkling your nose when you laughed. It was that which opened up the door of memory, and that giggle. Well, I suppose it is up to us to renew our relationship. Put me wise to this deal."

Then he remembered Marie[4], and said: "What will

---

[4] *Harry's wife.*

she do now, poor girl? She is about all in anyway, and now I have slid out of the game she will be not only all in, but heartbroken besides, for she loves me. How can I help her, Helen?" So we both went into the room with her upstairs when she was having such an awful time about her sleep. Then we went into the West Parlor, and Harry stood silent a long time beside his old body. "Poor devil," he muttered, as he looked. "What a thin old hulk it is! The marvel is how I managed the old machine so long."[5] Then he stretched his arms up and out and smiled at the sense of power and health he felt, and said: "Gee, Helen, isn't it just great to really live?' When you all came in so sweetly time after time to speak to him we stood and the tears flowed at the sight of such love and devotion. He said: "Helen, I wasn't worth all that; I couldn't have been. It's the sort of thing a saint ought to get, not a chap like me." He wanted to get into his old body just long enough to take you by the hand and thank you for it all. His face did reflect a bit of the love which welled up in his heart.

After it was all over, what a beautiful time we all did have with the music as we sat together. Sister felt us first, but all of you did before we left. Tee is very near to us both. His eyes almost see through, and his spirit is most beautiful; so is Papa's. You don't realize this now, but you will some day when he is all here, and can meet you as you come over, one by one. His is a hospitable spirit, and his will be the first to greet you after he is here. Harry and I can see that far ahead now.

[Harry continues the letter.] We stand here hand in hand, and it is good to have such a fine big sister to show me the ropes and help me to bear the separation from my own folks. You never can see or hear me when I sit among you and want to butt in on any little gab-fest you are having, nor can you

---

[5] *Harry died at age 33.*

realize how big and strong I look. I am rather struck by my looks. It is a long time since I looked like a real man, and I cannot help feeling fine over it. I cheer myself up, feeling my arms and legs, and finding them as hard as ever they were. What "gets my goat" still is how I can feel so firm and hard and material, and yet sail right through the sitting room wall or closed door. It keeps me wondering at the marvels of nature, for of course it is as natural and customary here as walking upstairs is with you. This getting-about game here has wireless skinned a million miles; it is so simple, seemingly, and so swift, and so altogether satisfactory. Yet I am the sub-freshman in a kindergarten class when it comes to really knowing anything about this place. I am too much interested in you all there to spend much time over the marvels here. They will keep, you won't; and I have a bit of sentiment about doing things over here with Papa in the party.[6] No one has to hurry here; we have time to burn, or rather no time at all; just a sort of continuous performance. I see you are tired, Sister, so thanks, and au revoir.

Goodbye from

HELEN and HARRY,
as Partners

---

[6] *Harry thought Papa would soon come over, and he wanted to wait to do things together with him. - L.E.B.*

22

ACCOUNTING FOR OTHERS . . . AND EARLY SPECULATION ABOUT REINCARNATION.

4

November 30, 1913

elen is here now, and Sister, always wait for me. I see you can feel a false hand at your side. Tell Papa we are both with him all the time; that every day Harry has work at his home, and I am working also, as is my habit, but we keep well in touch with Papa. We feel he is the nearest to us. We do all we know how to make his coming over as swift and sweet as Harry's was.

I cannot describe my own work as well as I wish I might, as it registers on the sort of material you are all unfamiliar with. Yes, that is bad grammar, I know, but it is not so easy to get one's best over. Conditions must be dealt with as well as may be.

F. met L., as he did his own boy. I was not there to see, but I believe his was not so happy a crossing as ours. We don't pry into these things here, but do only what is our special duty. Only the idle minds are curious about what is none of their concern. F. was with his mother when her other boy came over. I can tell you this much, that the latter came as a little child.[7] His mother has him to care for, and she feels she was much at fault for his present apparent age. She might have helped his soul to grow there, as she will do now here. Mothers always do what

---

[7] *He died a middle-aged man. L.E.B.*

they can here to rectify blunders made on earth. Mother-love is a most God-like attribute, and is a big factor in evolving the race.

Yes, I have seen Grandma B. She is beautiful too. Grandma E. is very beautiful here; tall and full of a grace she never had in her earthly body. She is so strong and sweet, and so full of love for all of us. She is always very near to Sister, whom she helps much. Grandma B. is rather smaller, but full of a certain quiet fun we all enjoy. Harry was more than delighted when I took him to her home.

Oh, yes, she has a home, surely, and in that will Papa first stay until he can build his own. Grandma E. has a home too, full of flowers which seem to be a part of herself. Grandma B. likes other things more. We all build for ourselves here, and for those who shall come after us; it is our recreation. Our work is done only for those who need, and to increase the fund of knowledge. Our playtime is home building, and we do put our best efforts into it. We study every detail, so that in all minute parts it shall be perfect, and fit those for whom it was builded.

Grandma B. lives in the lighter country where it is forever smiling summer; "Always May," she says. She has her boys about her, and some of them are very small.[8] Papa will help her bring them up; he is really her eldest now. Yes, you see we too have child souls here to watch over, and try what we can do, for a while. If we fail, then they are taken elsewhere to grow by other means.

I don't know, Sister, about reincarnation. Harry seems sure of it, and it may be so; we cannot disprove it. People do disappear from our ken here, as with you. Where they go we cannot tell. We speculate, of course, and we try hard to see when they go, and which way, but I, for one, have never been on hand when anyone I knew left here. Up or

---

[8] *All were grown men when they died. - L.E.B.*

down they might have gone; we can only surmise by
their looks. Some shrink and darken; some grow
larger, taller, and brighter. We guess, but we can
prove nothing. We have work to do, and pray to be
of the brighter bands who go. Common sense
suggests that with them one's chance is best. So we
work and wait for our dear ones, and are happy as a
rule.

HELEN

A SIGNATURE.

5

Note: Tee was taken very ill and we had to have two physicians and a blood specialist; also a trained nurse. The doctors could not diagnose the case, never having seen anything like it. On Sunday, when feeling a little eased of severe pain, Tee wished to try to get a message from his brother Hugh. The attempt was a failure. **L.E.B.**

h, Sister, you can't connect with anyone on a higher plane than ours because of the rates of vibration being so much more rapid. Only we "low-brows" can deal with you direct. Tell Tee that his brother is with him tonight, as his father said, and by results tomorrow he will see. Hughey is with Tee now, but is too bright a light for my dull person to be "comfy" with. J.S. Senior is hovering on the outskirts, but even he is in a class above us. Cheer up! There are plenty of classes here, scaled up literally out of sight. It's a big game, this life; real life, I mean. Makes a chap dizzy just to get a hasty look. There are so many more layers or zones than I ever could have imagined.

Gee, Sister, we are getting on fine. Tires you, I see. Never mind, it pleases me, and will be some stunt when we get it perfected. I should be helped to write if I could get over my own fist. I always was keen for that, you . . . , no, you don't know. I was about to say "you know," that classic sentence used by all civilized people. Helen isn't so keen on autographs as I am, so she puts in more time on ideas. Oh well, we'll cut it out for now as I see you are so tired. See if we can pull off some good signatures first. (His name in full and his town.) How's that, Sister? Ask Papa.

HARRY

Note: Sister had not been able to see well enough to read for years. Her vision had become impaired before her younger brother Harry was old enough to have learned to write, so she had really never seen his writing. Her handwriting was very coarse, so when Harry attempted to give a test of his personality by making her get his own handwriting which was very fine, it tired her extremely, and she was sure no one could read it, as it had seemed to her she was writing the letters over each other. When Harry finally did write his own name and city it was startlingly like his own hand, and was a convincing test to many, as she could not possibly have known what his handwriting was like, even had she wished to imitate it.

L.E.B.

ART IS ETERNAL, AND GOES RIGHT ACROSS THE BORDER CALLED DEATH.

6

December 13, 1913

ello, Tee: What gets my goat is that I have to rest up like a chap running to catch a car when I try to do this stunt. Ordinarily I feel like a two-year-old, but not at this game. Cigarette, bully! Enjoy yourself, Tee. Hit it up. It won't hurt him a bit, Sister. Let the autograph drop. Me for a gab-fest with Tee. You obliterate yourself, see!

Say, Tee, this is the best ever. If I only had a pal! The place is so full of doings. They are new and mighty interesting in detail. I am rather lonely just now for a friend and brother like Tee there. Join me? Rats, old man! Cut that idea till you've had a square deal where you are. Sit tight. Don't let anybody shove you off your own dump. It is a bully good dump at that. If you can be game to the finish, no matter what stumps are placed in your path, you can be one of the elect here all right, and when you figure that this is on the big time you are not going to make any bad bluffs at sticking to your work. What's the use of a man loving anything if it is not worth following any longer than he gets a crack at it over on your side of the fence? We feel here that if a chap has the grit to stick to any old thing till he cashes in, he stands a pretty decent chance of having his heart satisfied. What's the odds, Tee, whether stock you wanted is going to succeed or peter out? Its's a cinch *you* won't, anyway. Just believe your little brother Harry this much; you'll arrive O.K. there if it is in the cards. You have to tarry over a year, and if it is my good luck you join me here after that you will have no trouble getting all the work you want in this place.

Cheer up, Sister, he's not gone yet. Wet head! Dry up quick. You gum the game. Now, Tee, old man, take a brace, pull yourself up, and hit up the feed. Doc is too slow. Good old Doc, he did me many a fine turn, but he is slow. Shoot some genuine food at Tee, and see him blossom. Bacon, eggs, potatoes, and real meat; yes, steak. Gee, Tee, I sure hanker to take you out and tank you up a bit, as of yore. Remember how we hit it up that time you were here sick, at that grill joint, where the egg-nog was so superb? I can't help a dim regret when I let my mundane mind dwell on such low pastimes. I sigh for "them days" once in a while here; not for the booze or cigarettes, but for the fine feeling which went with them. Just to sit and "sodder," as it were, with the smoke curling upwards, and the thin glasses clinking with the ice, and the eyes of my brother shining with the love which outlives the body and the place and the time. I can feel that my time with you and Tee, is short; that the growing interest and feeling of inner strength will lure me further on. I too have a work. Don't know yet what it is, but I feel its grip in advance. No decent chap, no real man can loaf very long and keep his self-respect. I am marked for the laboring class. I see it coming.

Tee must cut out worry, fear, and discouragement, and believe in the dignity and use of what he has within to offer the public. He is on the right track to be able to continue here without breaking the thread as I had to do. Not business, but art is eternal, and goes right across the border called death. Thank God, you have had the sense to choose a real lasting work. Here I am, foot-loose, and at sea, with not an idea in my head as to a future. Had I only kept up my music or art I'd have had at least a start here. It's me for the employment bureau. Nothing doing. I've got to start at day labor under someone who has been wise elsewhere. If a chap could only know in advance what piffle he would land here with, only money in his hands, or rather in his head, and business methods! It's rest and a thinking part for him until he can get a line on some real work. I have a couple of rudiments,[9] that's true, but they are so very small it's me for a teacher, *muy pronto*.

Helen has been bully. She is such a big fine woman, better than any of us. She has a wholesome way of cheering me up, so I feel I can trust her to put me wise and on the right track.

Yes, Sister, this may be my last spiel for a while, but take it from me, love and work are all that cut any real figure anywhere. Live if you can, earn as you must, but keep heart and soul and mind free of the taint which comes of money-getting as an end. It is too absorbing to allow the development of the art work which lasts. What can we do here with anything else? Just service and study, that's the whole deal. Work and love are two other terms for the same idea. Be happy, no matter how the game turns. Be sure of my hearty welcome when you too arrive. Don't hurry. You can work there and find the place here ready and waiting.

Au revoir,

HARRY

---

[9] *Music and drawing.* - L.E.B.

VIBRATIONS . . .
HELPING THOSE WHO HAVE NOT
YET RUN THEIR COURSE.

7

December 15, 1913

ee is much better, Sister, and when we all are with him you ought to see what stunts we can do. Oh, we all take deep breaths of the air up here, then spread our hands over Tee, and watch the vital current run through him.

HARRY

This is Helen. Harry wasn't really strong enough to help Tee and write besides. Yes, it is queer about that, but we have a worse time trying to get words to you than we do to accomplish a tremendous amount of work over here. Harry is still a newcomer, and not entirely rhythmic yet. That only means his vibrations are jerky, which keeps him behind us when we are hastening to do some emergency work. Well, that sort of work means, as a rule, to join a circle banded together to help some sick person who hasn't run his course yet.

Do people die before their time? Yes, often; it happens to thousands. I mean people on your plane come here through accident or disease before they have built the bodies they need here.

Do you have to build your own body? Yes, you all build your future bodies, as we do our abiding places, and when one is hurled over too soon it is

31

not comfortable.

How is that? Oh, they cannot see, maybe or cannot hear, or perhaps are unable to move about. Yet, it is horrid, rather. That is why we all unite so readily to keep a soul in his body till we are sure he will arrive here in first-class condition.

I daresay it does seem queer to you to speak thus about the so-called dead, but we know it is very easy to arrange things here all right, and it gives us things to do while we remain on the plane near you. People come over sort of "half baked," Harry says. This side of our life interests Harry very much.

Well, to go back, when our circle is complete about Tee we take deep rhythmic breaths and then expel them in unison. This creates a steady flow of vital force from us through him, and then back to us again. If we are all very much in earnest and don't let ourselves be diverted by other people who like to meddle, we can always raise the resisting power of our patient, and his own force does the repair work. Tee should not be given any sort of "dope."[10] It is bad in every way, and prevents our getting to his center. It acts like a sort of smoke or cloud all about him. Harry says "tell Tee to cut it out.". . .

(Later.) No, F.H.[11] isn't here, not near us in any event. . . . No, we don't mingle. I don't know why. Yes, people of his faith take so long to shake off beliefs that it impairs their freedom as workers in the open field. Open field means to be able to respond to any call for help, no matter on what plane. It strikes us like a bell ringing. No, not loud, but penetrating. We always gather at the call if it is in any of our harmonics. Our own people register in

---

[10] *The doctors had been giving him morphine.-L.E.B.*

[11] *Father Hughes, a Paulist priest. In a later letter (37 in this printing), early judgments about Father Hughes are amended.*

some harmonic of your personal tone or sound vibration. When we hear any bell tone belonging in our key we stop what we are doing and drift swiftly towards it, or let our magnetic sense carry us instead of our will. It always takes us more swiftly than anything else. When all respond to a call they recognize one another as a family group.

Those of Father Hughes' faith form groups apart working for their own. Father Hughes is still with that group.

Isn't he beyond that yet?

No, he believes he belongs there, but later he will realize the common call as we do. Yes, they are good; it is not that which binds them close, but belief which holds them captive to a smaller area of usefulness. Help Tee now. *Au revoir.*

(Later.) Yes, Sister, we have concluded to let Tee's brother come again, as he is so much more powerful than any of us. Of course he wants to help, but the laws are such here that he cannot unless we all make links in the chain of Tee's friends and relatives. Yes, father and all; father makes the first link. Yes, that is it, the bridge; and we act as reducers, Harry being next to Tee. There are ten of us. With a perfectly harmonious chain we can do a great deal, provided Tee helps by being relaxed in his mind; that is, feeling certain of our help. This mental attitude makes the first link strong enough to carry more vital force than it could if he were just despondent or discouraged. We must have connections all along the line, which are strong. Mental color can harm or help to a vast degree. Mental color is the term we use here for mood. In truth it is merely a higher or lower rate of vibration.

HELEN

GAINING POWER THROUGH UNSELFISH WORK.

8

December 17, 1913

arry is with you now. Notice how much faster I write now? Helen is off on one of the emergency cases she told you about. Oh, I don't know who is in trouble; it is some family party she is mixed up with. She has a great many friends, and it is some of them. Being only more or less of a looker-on, I am not in on her trips elsewhere. I sit round and watch old Tee. Tell him he can bet on his little brother Harry sitting tight till he passes up all doctors.

Oh, I loaf round him, sitting on the bed, or close by. I wish I could let Tee in for a good old-fashioned talk, the sort with plenty of pauses drifting along through it. I wish he could get my voice, even as near like it as this writing.

Helen is nothing if not a hustler. She has the busy bureau beaten to a finish, always going. Yes, Sister, I seem to be doomed to snag up against the people who work in places I cannot loaf in. I have a sneaking hunch that before long the work bug will begin to burrow into me also. I begin to feel a deep stirring desire to get busy. I feel so well and strong and fine it seems only decent to get into line and lend a boost where it is needed. Tell old Tee I am using him as "the dog" to try it on. If I make good where I can throw into the job so much heart, maybe I can help a person elsewhere who is simply needy. There is no hurry over here; one can take all the time he needs to decide just the sort of thing he wants to begin on. I never was one to sweat the steers when it came to deciding any vital question.

HARRY

Harry has gone to rest. This is Helen. I will tell you about V. She is in a beautiful home of her own, with her husband and child. I have not taken Harry yet, as his eyes are not strong enough to bear the light which shines there. He will gain his powers as soon as he begins to take part in the unselfish work.

No, we never tell anyone this. It must come from within. He begins to feel the stir of it already, but there is no hurry. He will soon find his own center and begin to generate power greater than he needs for his own use. When once he can realize that he will commence work. As yet he only believes it is the old, natural vitality returned. Soon he will begin to see that it is something else, and will wonder what it is; what splendid driving force lies within him, and then the light will break, and his soul will respond in the big way his can. His will be a tremendous power, once his mind, soul, and heart are linked. Trinity it is. Mysterious and subtle; mind, heart, and soul. It is the unison of the three in perfect balance which Tee's brother has, and that is why he lives at such a tremendous rate of vibration. Saints are only just that. Theirs is the life in the Golden Country, where the sunshine is brilliant, yet soft as moonlight.

HELEN

A SQUARE DEAL . . .
YOU YOURSELF ARE
JUDGE AND JURY.

9

December 24, 1913
Christmas Eve

ello Pal: I see you have bucked up, and are almost back at the mines. It is too early to predict what sort of job I land, but it is a cinch it won't be easy. I realize daily I have grown rusty while sick, and while I feel. bully I am not what I wish I were. No one is that, I suppose, but I seem particularly useless, just a big husky loafer. Sure thing, when I find what I can do maybe I can get another note to you, but this communication stunt eats up energy like a boat race or a gruelling contest of any sort, and besides it is hard on Sister, lots harder than she realizes, so cannot afford to waste myself or her in just pleasant converse. I realize I must make a career for myself as an excuse for being alive. I must either make good at something or go into the discard. Don't know how or what that is exactly, but you get me. Make good I must; make good I wish to; and I have a hunch it is not so easy here as it looks at first. I cannot even get a look-in where your brother lives and enjoys working. He is so far above us I feel ashamed. What a mean, selfish cuss I must be when a chap like him out-classes me so far I cannot even look at him.

Your little brother Harry has done some tall self-examination of late, and is wise to quite a few points of his makeup he wasn't on to before. That is one satisfaction, Tee; you can sit and think until hell freezes over, and no one is at all annoyed at your leisurely processes.

On the whole, this is the place for a square deal. You get what is yours, and get nothing more nor less. Some of us are a bit peeved now and then, but one can't put up a kick, as the boss of the works isn't visible, or rather, between us, you yourself are judge and jury. That is the slick part of the arrangement. Self accused, you have no escape. You get a true line on your own past, your own true motives, and this innate force within does the rest. I can't but admire the simplicity and the lack of waste of the plan. Omar is right: "Thou, thyself art heaven and hell." Think of the labor saving device it is. The system sets a soul free, leaves it alone, and the contained ingredients do the rest. Can you beat that, say? I must stop now. I see Sister is all in. So am I, if it's not impolite to state it. Here's to you, now and always.

HARRY

THE LAW . . .
AND GUARDING AGAINST
LEAKS IN VITALITY.

10

Christmas, 1913

 promised to write once more. It's not Harry but Helen who writes. Harry is not strong enough for a long letter, and we both feel Sister can't endure the drain he puts on her. I have more vigor to give, so I don't need to use such a lot of Sister, see?

We want to tell you about the life here, as we feel it's wise or useful to you all. When we say we are not permitted, we don't mean to say some outsider refuses consent, but that we ourselves feel it either unwise or ungenerous to tell certain things. Your brains have limits beyond which we dare not lead you, as the substructure of your habitual thought won't bear it. Foolish people here have often, from both kind and unselfish motives, brought on insanity to those they wished to help most, so we grow cautious.

I have often seen Tee's brother, and am his pupil on the violin, as well as in experimental work with nature forms in music. He is one of our great music masters here, and it was on his plane I spent most of my time since I wrote before. His home is higher than mine, but I can study there with benefit, as it has a tremendous uplifting power. I have arranged that Harry shall be a student with him, just as soon as he has prepared himself to enter. One goes through regular tests before such entrance, such as one must pass before entering any other art or study. The tests differ of course, and are almost all character strains; tests of nerve, will, of benevolence, of charity, and of constructive force. The student may take all the time needed to pass, or to prepare himself. Harry will do well, of course, as soon as he rids himself of his most prominent limitations. I don't feel it wise or kind to tell what these are. Here is Harry at last. He was off with M. while I was doing this part of our joint letter.

HELEN

Here I am, folks, feeling particularly fit. I feel a heap more cheerful since I know I am to be a pupil with Tee's brother, and under my big sister Helen's wing. Helen is taller than Sister, and looks like her picture a bit, but has a glorious coloring, and hair long as well as curly. Cheer up, Sister; you shall have long hair too, up here; just as big a wad as you wish; that is provided always that you pass your character tests. It isn't so disheartening either as it seems at first, since you aren't hustled or worried about the other fellow's marks. Competition is eliminated here. One wrestles with one's inner enemy, the selfish self. Therefore, one spends all one's energy on a concentrated effort to improve and qualify for the upper class. The worst is past when one comprehends the general drift of the system. I begin to realize the marvels of the simple system, and grow reverent and humble as I get a glimpse of its beauty and justice. Lucky you can't see it, or you'd never tarry to finish the game. Your work there is like trying to carve ivory with an axe. Your intentions may be noble, but the workmanship is coarse. I am only too thankful I came when I did, though it was long before I was needed here, and so I must remain a student until my life clock should have run down of its own accord. I came here for a fault of my own, and for that mistake I must pay

39

the price "The Law" requires of ignorance as well as insight.

Tee is right in his instinct to cut out every atom which will cloud or dim his senses, as he must do all of his "prep" school work there if he possibly can, in order to enter the man's class here. He should guard his vitality at all its points of leakage, even overwork. Even that counts against him here. Guard your highest power, Tee, and if you carefully watch all small leaks, you can do all required to earn your bread and cheese. It's always the unnoted drains or leaks, the dribble, which empties the reservoir in the end; never the legitimate call. Ponder on this, Tee, for the sake of our living comradeship. I am not preaching, just giving you a time, as man to man.

HARRY

OLD KATE . . .
BLACK AND WHITE ARE NOT
SKIN COLORS HERE.

11

December 29, 1913

o you wish me to tell you about old Kate? She is as white as any of us here. No, most beautiful, with a shining body and hair. She is one of us here who is helping you there. Yes: Negroes don't exist here. Why? Because souls are either good or bad, and good means always bright or white.

Black G's soul is wonderful. He doesn't seem to have any dark spots at all. He serves singing. By that we know the elect, or chosen ones, who rise at once to the bright country; those who service is given with a glad heart. It's the mark of nobility here to be one of the "singing souls."

Dark souls indicate selfishness, greed, and crime. Crime means here self-destruction by disregarding others entirely. That makes one blacker than murder. Murder may be done through an instant's insanity, but selfishness eats deeply and steadily at the root of life itself. It can wither a beautiful body like fire, and darken and distort till the soul looks almost inhuman or unhuman.

Negroes have frequently far brighter bodies here than those they served there.

Never forget this, and watch the secret creeping growth of selfishness as if it were a smouldering fire, eating into the home, by stealth, while you

41

make merry. Selfishness and greed are the only real destructive things I have seen here.

Goodnight,

HELEN

THE BRIGHT COUNTRY HIGHER UP . . . TRUTH IS THE MOST WITHERING THING IN THE UNIVERSE.

12

January 4, 1914

e want to tell you how Harry is getting on. He went up with me to the bright country where our music master lives. Harry had an awfully hard time to manage with his eyes. Oh, it is so much lighter than any other light he had ever experienced, and so much more depressing. Why? Because I forced his entrance before he was properly fitted for it, and he experienced a shock when he took the first look into his own heart. I felt he was strong in his mind, and I was so very happy to have him with me, and so longed to get him to work that I let him take the plunge; though I knew what he hadn't learned, that the higher one rises here the more transparent [becomes] one's self-protecting veil of ignorance about oneself. I took the long chance, both because he wished it, and because I did. I never happened to be with anyone before when the light of self-revelation broke over him. If I had I should have hesitated some time before running such a risk. Harry came through bravely, as I knew he would, but it was awful; awful in a way none of you there can realize. He went blind at first, and just crumpled up like a wilted flower. Truth is the most withering thing in the universe, and it requires the greatest courage to face the truth about oneself. No matter how humble we fancy ourselves, the discovery awaits us that we are

43

more arrogant than anyone we ever met. When revelation comes it sets out every detail of our lives with a clean-cut distinctness no eyes can mistake, no charity cover. Each soul must face himself alone at some time; look, see, and judge. Then, however prostrated, rise and begin to fight his way up toward perfection, undaunted and fearless, with hope as well as courage.

Harry met his trial, faced it, and after the shock rose up with the courage that was always his. When he felt the light breaking his eyes closed, and for a while he felt sure he was blind for good and all, but I was near enough to reassure him, and his own strength did the rest. Now we are both students with the master, Tee's brother. Harry will first play the piano until he can move up to the handling of tone color. He has a most wonderful comprehension of the relation of things. His work with piano will lead him beside me, so we can do creative and experimental work together. It was for this we both agreed to risk his coming here so soon. Harry's love of his own is so strong he couldn't bear the idea of separation from me for so long. This work with the master is of course only part of what we do. We belong to the band who follow the open field work, and we, like all of that band, respond to the "common call" for help. Harry is so delighted to be "in it" as he says, and is gaining poise so rapidly that life here is a constant delight in spite of the separation in a way from you. Now that we are really no longer apart we have very little to cloud our perfect happiness.

HELEN

SMALL POWERS OF
LOVING ARE WHAT
DESTROY BODIES.

13

Evening, January 4, 1914

es, Sister, it is I. Helen has told all about the stunt higher up. I can feel that, although, I wasn't at hand myself. Somehow, I begin to feel older and more serious. That word "stunt," for instance, does not fit at all. It was the most momentous instant, or eternity (I can't say which even now) of my up-to-now recalled existence. Hell, as you imagine it, is a mild and milky term to express a reality like the one I still marvel I survived. Helen's faith in me was firm, or I could never have come through with my senses left. No use dreading it, Mamma. That won't help a bit, and it simply weakens the resisting power besides. Just put your house in order as swiftly as possible, and cut out everything you can see there as unworthy. Then when your moment comes it will be not only easier, but less prostrating. I never clogged myself with possessions, God knows; but even with that handicap off I nearly went under for keeps.

Mamma wants to know whether my smoking did not cut the largest figure in my destiny there. No, it did nothing of the sort. It was lack of faith and courage, and a self pity that did the tissue-breaking which caused death. Once and for all get the idea out of your head that any appetite or indulgence cuts a big figure in any destructive way here. It merely affects the body there, and only that because

45

it is in connection with mental and spiritual destructive forces. I cannot put this too emphatically, not only for Mamma, but for all of you. One fit of temper, for instance, can break down more healthy cells in the body than a year's smoking or eating or drinking; because, and note this carefully, the forces of mental and spiritual elements are as a thousand to one of the physical ones. Depression, cowardice, in all their forms, are more potent than T.B. germs at their most riotous moments. This fact hides the secret of all so-called New Thought and Christian Science cures. They try to teach the full subservience of physical matter to spirit or soul quality. These qualities are about as close together, say, as a rock and a man; a lumbering ox or elephant cart beside the latest automobile. Don't class at all, in fact. When doctors will quit studying germs, and begin to study characteristics and temperaments, they will come a heap nearer the goal they seek. Gloom, pessimism, fear, discouragement, hopelessness; these are what kill people, not the so-called disease. Bad temper, harsh judgements, lack of patience, and small powers of loving are what destroy bodies.

Look well to the spirit of intolerance, all of you. Live and let live; fight and let fight. Every fellow has a full-sized job of his own on hand if he only knew it. One ought not to waste one ounce of power in criticism; he needs all he has, and then some, to meet and grapple with his own problems. This doesn't mean just Mamma and her smoke mania; it means each and all. There is no one who doesn't waste more or less time passing judgment on somebody else's faults or weaknesses. If we all could realize that every word or thought in such a case acts as a weight hung about our own necks, a weight we must free ourselves from before we can join any decent society here, we would keep a watch on ourselves that would soon bring joy all along the line, as well as health and power.

I suppose I take a chance in telling all this, but I want, if possible, to help you from the awful hole I

46

was in, and it can do no harm. Look closely to your own habits, your thoughts, and see what can be profitably eliminated. One must come over here light. Light means in all senses. I begin to see truth in the Bible I never noticed before. Those old fellows got wise to the game. "Lay not up treasures on earth," etc. I'm short on quotation, but you recall the idea. The treasures were to be laid up over here where they had some true value. Earth values are so false. They almost overlook entirely what lasts, what moulds the universe, which is human character. That's the answer to everything: character. It has nothing to do with property, or possessions so-called. B's true value, that is, what his money means to him, is just being an honest man; that's what he brings here, and it is all he brings of what he calls his wealth, and he could have had the same place here without one cent in his purse, or a bond in the bank. "An honest man": that's nobility enough. That's the hallmark. These may gather from diverse quarters; any who have worked and been honest, whether for salary, income, or wages, it makes no difference whatever. Even one's garments here are made from one's quality of character. I am only glad mine are not quite black. I can assure you they are not white, though happily lighter than when I came. Sometimes I am wild to tell all I have found out; then I wonder if it would do any real good. Perhaps; I can't say.

HARRY

47

ABOUT CREMATION
AND EMBALMING.

14

January 8, 1914

ister: About the cremation. I didn't feel it at all, nor did Helen, but there are those here who say it is not as comfortable a way to come over as being buried. Why? Well, I fancy it breaks up tissue roughly, but so far as any of us are concerned, we believe it a safer way to destroy the body than to risk being attached to it too long. A lingering disease so loosens all the particles of the body that the envelope is slipped out of easily. With others, who for any reason are too closely knit together, it is painful, but at worst it is only for a few moments or seconds, and if a person has any spirit at all worthwhile it is a blessing to be so swiftly separated.

Here there are as many opinions regarding cremation as with you, both for and against, according to individual experience or preference. A slow, patient temperament dislikes it. To such it seems too much like being "yanked" over here, while with me I am only too glad to feel it was done. I don't hanker to tarry long away from my own. So far as I can see, it is about a stand-off, with the balance, if any, in favor of cremation, there being only discomfort in that, and no risk. What do I mean by risk? Well, when a soul and body separate too gradually the soul has to stay on a low plane, peopled with the scum of life. These often amuse

48

themselves by torturing the soul with all sorts of ingenious tales as to their whereabouts. These low souls are frequently very clever and can fool the ignorant new arrival, and hamper his unfoldment. He knows nothing, usually, of what he is up against, and they play upon his credulity and keep him from coming higher as long as they can. Do you get me? Besides, the crematory is never a gathering place for harpies. They are better amused in graveyards, which remind me that there is a reason for so many primitive minds fearing a graveyard. It is the instinctive shrinking from contamination, for these places are filled with the worst elements here, crowded. The embalmed bodies last so long that frequently their souls are tied there, and so make sport for the vicious-minded here. It is one of our missions to go to places of that sort, and fight for the decent people there. The weak or vicious dead we cannot help, they are among their own and must suffer, so you can well see why I far prefer cremation.

Tell C. her feelings were not the counterpart of what we must suffer, but that she was the victim of obsession. She is so mediumistic that she is a prey to any trick some of us here care to play. Tell her to set her will against all demonstrations of any sort from this side, and she will grow much stronger. She has had her vitality drained for years by souls from this side. If she will take herself in hand at all points, and keep her will against all forms of mediumship she will find she has a wonderful constitution. Those who live on her surplus vitality are members of her own family over here. They are the mean ones, of course, and they should be stopped. Helen and I have talked over plans to help her free herself, and we think we can help her if she will aid us from her side.

HARRY

49

DR. M. . . .
VICTIMIZED BY THE
SPIRIT WORLD.

15

January 17, 1914

ister: I will try to answer the question you wanted to ask for J.[12] I have seen Dr. M. We had some mutual work to do in the matter of our personal relations. I misjudged him, and of course had a strong desire to repair my fault. The doctor is working hard, and is one of the big helpers over here along his own lines. He was far too easily influenced from this side toward the later years of his life, and so fell into the power of the unscrupulous souls so thick over here. Because of the obsession of this man here, the doctor, who has a splendid strong soul, was victimized, and almost swept away from his moorings. It was the wonderful devotion of his friend, J., which saved his soul as well as his body. For this service Dr. M. is doing all he can here, and wishes me to have you tell J. that he will see to it he never has any long illness there before he passes over. He shall come through swiftly, and without pain of any sort. With this love working for him here, he need never worry over future trouble. "I know how to repay great service," tell him, "and he may count on my help always."

If J. will let you tell him about what you have already had from me, he will gain a fair idea of

---

[12] *J. was a dentist.*

conditions here. The influence which tried to wreck Dr. M. was from one who had followed his life for years. Thanks to J. he has been absolutely eliminated. Dr. M. says he tries always to prevent J. from taking up with any mediums, as he now realizes why it was so disastrous for him. He let down the bars of his splendid will, and so laid himself open to the fate which almost got him. Sister, do not write much; it is too risky. Just as soon as any of the unscrupulous find out you are open to our vibratory connection they will try to push us away, and replace us, using you to their own ends. You are already easy, and for that reason be careful. I am working daily on the plane Helen told you about, so cannot come to you as quickly or easily as before. Because of this fact it is a danger that unscrupulous spirits can profit by. Only when you have some really vital question to ask allow yourself to write. Otherwise wait until one of us causes you to feel impelled to, as today. I find you always feel my will, so there is no danger of losing our connection.

Au revoir,

HARRY

BRIDGING THE GULF . . .
HARRY'S ASCENSION.

16

February 8, 1914, Helen's birthday

ister: Here I am, Helen. I was going to come anyway today, as I have news for you. Harry has gone up with Hugh, Tee's brother, to stay all the time, so he cannot come to you again unless I come too, because when his vibrations have risen to the standard required there, he will lose his power to link himself to you without a reducer. Yes, that is why I stay on this lower plane so long, in order to be able to help you when you need me most. Harry has risen so fast he has already lost much of his power to connect with you. He wants to write Tee once more before the door closes his free speech. Of course he will serve you all there, as I do here, but he cannot talk to you or answer questions directly, as I do.

Thanks for the flowers, they warm the heart. Isn't it splendid Harry can live with the master? It is really nothing for me to stay behind. I can be there later. Time is nothing to us here. I am always busy, always happy anywhere. I may still stay there part of the time. This birthday is to be Harry's day of entrance into the glad country of the bright sun where life and work are more intense, more selfless, so it is our double birthday. Sister, you must not write any more now.

My love to you all, as ever.

HELEN

52

Dear Mamma: It is I, Harry. I leave today to live with the master. I wish to say just a word, *entre nous*, before I go into the higher life work. See if you can get into a state of mind where it is easier to give than to keep or take. If you can learn that one thing, all else will be easy. "Easier to give than to take or keep." That's all. It is a mental trait, and your mind will do what you ask of it.

Helen today gives up her opportunity to enter the higher life because if she did there would be no link between us. I have never seen a nobler sacrifice. Helen has a generosity past belief. Her love for us all is as bright as a ray of pure sunlight. We should all feel the inspiration of her loving sacrifice. You can hear of me through Helen often enough to bridge the gulf. It is only an *au revoir*, Mamma. We shall all be here in a little while. I know by what is in me that you will rise to your duty, and learn your individual lesson.

With the love which has no death,

Your boy,

HARRY

Helen's birthday is mine.

(Later)

Sister, I am here, Harry. First it is a word to dear old Tee. I want him to know where I shall be from today on. It is with your brother, Tee, whom we call the master. I am fortunate enough to have qualified there, and I shall try to live on his plane. I have the strength to endure, and please God, I shall hold up my end there as befits a man. You, my brother, shall be one of us when the time comes, but do not try to come until you can take your own work here, as it is too uncertain. I feel I only got in by a special effort of the master, and more for your sake than my own. He loves you Tee, so deeply that the

53

light of it blesses all whom you care for as well. What we shall do, and the method of it, is so far from methods, as well as means, with you, that it is fruitless to explain.

One thing I wish to impress on you is to stick close to your wife. In her animal magnetism you have a fountain of the sort of force you lack. She gives freely, without depleting her own strength, and you need her. Have no fear that it is unfair to her. It is a part of her work to supply this lack of your magnetism. You see, in your work you give more than you can generate, whereas with her, she generates more than she herself can use. It is one of the economies of nature, this balance between husband and wife. Without her supply you cannot do your best. She dislikes writing this, but it is I speaking, not she herself. I have no other line of communication open.

Stick to your present line, Tee. Stick, no matter what the barriers are. It is the road to Hughey. Never forget that. Use every material advantage put in your way. Guard your life as a sacred thing. Watch all leaks, all waste. Express art in as many forms as you like, but do nothing which does not bear in one way or another on the main subject, dramatic expression through personality. That is it. Human experiences made to express some hope, some form of development. It will grow into the work here step by step. Keep faith with us, your two brothers; keep faith with your highest ideals. Leave all the small things in their true relative positions, and with faith in your work, faith in yourself, and faith in us here, you will do your part in the one work there. I feel this is my last talk with you directly. When my vibrations are raised to a uniform rate I shall lose the power to write through Sister, as she will then need a reducer between us. Helen, with her big, unselfish heart, gives up her fuller life here in order to keep the way open between us. Hers is one of the most generous natures I have ever seen.

One thing more before I go. Remember that

Hughey and I need the dramatic art to complete the work we plan to do together. Get all you can there for the sake of our future combined effort to develop a fuller, higher art here. Each can give a different experience, equally of value to the new product. Complete your own portion there, carrying it as far as possible, not only in the technique, but in the spirit of it, in its ethical phase. Study the cause and effect of certain plays on different classes, and study also methods of graduated developers of brain power and moral sense. Try leading the ignorant along pleasant by-ways to unconscious planes of moral strength. We strong are "Our brother's keeper." It is up to us to lead him out of the gray twilight of moral and mental inaction into the sunlight of intelligent moral consciousness, and self-conscious effort to better living. It is up to you, old man. It is up to us all. It is all we are here for, just to help. That is the keynote of the universal song. We give and we take help. Bury pride. Vanity has no place in our work. Use the tools presented, but keep the idea clear before you. Give, take, work, and be glad. It is a man's game. It is worth while, Tee.

Adios,

HARRY (Your brother, and Hughey's brother, too)

FALSE MESSAGES FROM HARPIES AND VAMPIRES.

17

Note: The first part of this letter was lost in transmission because of the invasion of other influences during its communication.
L.E.B.

Undated

hen people receive messages from here you are helpless to determine who the senders are, so it is only by the character of the contents of each message that you can have any feeling of security that the person whose name is attached is giving the message.

Rose's mother[13] has been for years on a very high plane. But . . . and this you must note well . . . there have been none able to take her messages before we came and completed the chain of love from here to there. It takes love, and those who care, to make the chain strong enough to carry past the borderland of darkness where spirits live who love to deliver false messages from us to you. We feel even more strongly than you the injustice of this arrangement. It is one of the laws we resent

---

[13] *Henry Blount's first wife. Rose was a half-sister.*

and cannot understand, this being unable to prevent
inferior personalities from linking themselves more
readily with you than we who wish only good, and
never misuse the power given one of you to make
the link with us here. We sometimes have to fight to
keep the harpies and vampires away from those we
love, because our people are so ignorant they allow
themselves to drift below the boundary line where
we always conquer. We must be very, very strong in
spirit to be able to vanquish the low when they are
on our plane. We must have been here long, and
have wiped from our own hearts all lower qualities
in order not to risk being at least crippled by a
band of the strong lower souls. Were we high enough
to easily conquer them we should then be unable to
connect with you. See how it works? Those who
remain on the border are subject to the ills this
plane has. We, as well as you, must pay a price for
all we enjoy. Rose's mother can now send a message
direct through Harry and me. We have chains now in
many direction, quite complete. Rose has no more
loving or loyal helper than her own sister Josie, who
was only a baby when she came over, and so has
more knowledge of this place than of your plane.
She has a nature more like her mother's than Rose's,
yet she is so sweet and bright she can penetrate
into darker places than we dare to go, and can help
direct us as to what is best to do in certain crises
of your lives. We try to protect our own plane from
evil influences. Josie is D.[14]'s best protector. Her
love keeps off all evil thought directed toward him.
She has helped to keep his mind clean and pure as
Rose has. Mothers must sleep sometimes, and cannot
always be there to protect their beloved ones. We
watch over them while she sleeps, or is occupied
with other duties. We have the advantage of being
able to see evils approaching. Rose's mother directs
us many times, and shows us where and how to give

---

14 *A nephew.*

the help she cannot herself perform. Oh, it is all a big, splendid system for helping. Harry told it. It is just give and take help, give with love, take with gladness.

Sister, don't worry about any of the things we have you write. Fred[15] is quite right about testing us well. Why should you resent that if you have the feeling that precludes the real test? There must be sympathy or the chain breaks.

Goodbye,

HELEN

---

[15] *A half-brother.*

ENTHUSIASM IS
A LIFE GIVER.

18

March 13, 1914
At New York City

he oozing out of vigor of life and joy is a deadly thing to allow to continue. It is one of the points of leakage Harry mentioned in Tee's letter. Enthusiasm is a life giver. It means a speeded or lifted vibration, and that means more life current, more power.

Both Tee and you should watch that, and when you see things beginning to drag, do something new. Keep your life current at its best, and good of all sorts will come. That one thing is absolutely essential to Tee's work. He is too apt to take what comes, letting himself drift instead of taking a vigorous hold on circumstances, and changing the rate of his own vibrations. He could help his own lowered condition by going about to shows, but the other way is better, as it helps John[16] up also. The unselfish thing is always best when possible. The machine will pull all of you up higher. That is what I have wanted to say ever since you came, but you wouldn't let me.

I am glad always to see you hesitate, as it means you will be safe from others. It is more difficult to connect with you in the city, as you will guess, and

---

[16]*Thurlow and Mary's son, John Sargent White.*

I must often renew my strength from Harry who helps me that way. He is so full of life now, and so eager to help Tee and you. We will write a letter on your wedding anniversary.

With love from both,

HARRY AND HELEN

TRUE VALUES
CAN MELT TROUBLES
LIKE A SNOW BANK IN JULY.   **19**

April 6, 1914
At New York City

elen is here. This is the day we promised
to write again. First, Harry wants to tell
Tee that he has been with the master
constantly since we last wrote, and that things have
opened up for him; that he is wild to get over to
Tee as it would enable him to master his own
problem so easily. But he has learned also that one
can no more force another's experience than one can
force open a flower before it is ready and willing to
open itself.

Harry has thought hard to find some way to help
Tee get away from his present impediment, but he is
baffled at all points. Harry says it is the eternal
game of seek and find for oneself. The only hint we
can give is just to harp on what all other teachers
from the beginning have harped on. Love and
service, faith and a serene trust. Those are all terms
as dead as doornails unless one has seen the answer.
Deep down in the heart of all lies the key to
success, no matter what sort, but none but self can
use it and none but self can locate it. That is the
difficulty as well as the justice of it. With the best
intent, and a constant effort to find the hidden
push-button which frees our power, we must grope
alone.

Tee has intuition, so have you. Each must follow

61

his own. We were both so sure the buying of the car would help, but even we hadn't reckoned on your mental attitude, which would have blocked any good in the thing itself. You see it is hard for us here to realize the real weight of material standards with you. We see moral and mental conditions so far outweigh money or its equivalent that we feel with a distinct shock their hold over you there. This fact we must reckon with, or rather you must. It seems childish, even silly to us, these conventional standards about things. If you could only for one illuminating instant get a look at true values as they exist here, all your troubles would melt like a snow bank in July.

Then, we say, what next? We must help you in some way. We must still have some ideas in common. We can't allow ourselves to degenerate into a bureau for information as to the location and status of relatives and friends passed from your sight. Life is too big and serious a matter for that. What we want to do is to get some idea across which will the quicker solve the problems which material conditions daily present: Some glimmer of the big, eternal law we all live in. That is the question we ponder. It is as truly a problem as it would be for a land animal to instruct a fish how to develop lungs and legs. It resolves itself into how to accelerate evolution. It's a matter of growth. The impulse of growth is desire: life, aspiration, what you will. When the desire is intense enough it will create conditions. Creation comes from within us. Exterior agents assist only casually, as the sun helps to open the bud. The desire to open comes from within, and it can and will open without the sun, but the sun quickens the ultimate result. Fundamentally, the desire, the impulse must be strong at the center of being.

Success in any work depends upon how much we really love that thing. The more strongly we feel, the surer we are of success or achievement. Impediments are the cross currents of mental attitudes which will deflect the general direction and retard results. One's eye must be single to any success. Not so selfishly single as worldly success demands, but single as to the sweeping aside of all personal vanity or petty feeling.

One may love an art, and yet only sacrifice oneself to achieve success there. The element of sacrifice seems one of the inevitable ingredients or elements of real success. However, we sacrifice too easily material things, holding back the sacrifices of our personal habits or mental traits, or our ideas. We can part with anything sooner than with our own set mental states, wrong though they be by every higher standard of ethics. Our ideas of what is right and proper we cling to long after they can be proved false and useless. One almost despairs of being able to do anything for those on the material plane. If your ideas were as fluidic as ours, if you let go of your preconceived notions as easily as we do, you could forge ahead by leaps and bounds. A hot blast of suffering sometimes melts you up, when reason could chip away for years at some idea and never dislodge it. It would be funny if it were not so near tragedy, this tenacity of ideas. A new idea is as hard to get accepted as any fact in nature. Our only comfort lies in the effect which coming here produces on so many of you. Having been obliged to see you had a mistaken idea about death, makes it possible to give hospitality to other new and startling facts.

One's mind must be as open as a child's to profit by teaching, no matter on what plane of life. An open mind and a hospitable heart are what we all must have to secure more than we have of anything. Harry says that Tee must follow his own inner light and work on his personal defects, with the idea of getting his whole mental and spiritual system loosened up, just as he would work on a stiff muscle.

Kick over conventional standards of conduct, make a set of his own wherein selfishness is the only sin; a desire to do and be his best, his only impulse. It really cuts very little swath what color the flower be, just so it opens up; opening up at this stage of the game being the one object to strive for. Let us look deep within and see what we really love most, then go after it. The primal impulse must be strong to push through obstructions. The obstructions are there to test its strength merely. Few of us know what we really desire. When we do we arrive, because desire is the great creator. Desire and love. There isn't a thing on earth as strong as these. All bend before and beneath them.

What work do you love, and why? Ask yourself that, and see that you answer truthfully. An unworthy desire has death in its success. It may come up to the barrier, even from unworthy work earnestly pursued. But at the barrier the unworthy is left behind. Here the idea with the big thing behind it only can enter and grow and develop. Not the work, but what we feel about the work gives it its desirable quality; makes it worthy the larger life; makes it able to withstand the disintegrating process of more rapid vibration. Without some percentage of eternal stuff or living matter no idea or work can pass into the more stable realm we live in.

You know that certain elements with you disintegrate with heat. A very little heat will spoil meat or vegetable matter, while metals will stand much. The law holds along the line from cabbages to friendship. Many give way under certain adverse conditions. If they pass these tests they are made of the right material, and will retain individual life. Our mistake is in labeling the transient with the mark of the permanent. Love or friendship not based on unselfishness surely crumbles at the test.

Everything has its place. The wise enjoy each in its place, use it and pass on. Tell Mamma that we can see our dear ones if we choose, but earth ties soon resolve themselves into comradeships with work as a common bond. Those who live at our vibratory rate are our comrades unless a great love has linked us there, in which case we serve those if they are beneath us, and they are thus helped by us to lift themselves higher here.

A few simple rules are enough to help anyone to right living. Get them down to simple primary impulses, and all you need is time, to arrive. It's easy when you know how, like walking, or breathing, or loving. A step at a time, one breath at a time. Love first close to one's heart, then in ever widening circles until it includes all life. It is too simple. The mind shoots past the mark, hunting difficulties.

First causes are always simple. Take life, for instance, a life germ. What is it? A tiny, invisible something, yet so powerful, so wise it can build a tree, or a man, or a world about itself. We sometimes feel we have solved the eternal question when we say the vital spark is Love, because we can see what power that force has here. It seems able to create, though of course there may be something behind that. Harry and the master and I often discuss it, and try to prove our position by creating some wonderful fabric, or work of music with that force only. The master thinks it is only one of the aspects of creative principle, but low in the scale of souls as we are, we can do wonderful things with it. Elements and feeling here are interchangeable terms. Substance also can be resolved back and forth from one to another; tone into color, form into tone, and back again. One learns to build an idea into many forms of expression, the idea only remaining the same.

Of course you know it's the artist who is permanent, not the form of his work. The artist is the personification of a permanent idea or attitude. He may use any material he likes; could do so always if he but knew it; make music, or machines, or pictures, or cook and serve a meal without impairing at all his personality as an artist, or a creator of feeling-producing work. Anyone who creates anything with his heart in his work is an artist, and capable, after preparation, of creating other things. One must belong to the creative class or death ensues. Rewards have nothing to do with it as such. Every one must produce something of his own. You can easily see that living under different conditions, we must work each in his own way, and explanations are futile. Essential things we discover, each for himself, having the key. A numberless throng have found the way to swifter progressive life. Swift or slow, it matters very little, so we move on an upward slant. Lucky the one who can do his work singing. It's the sun to the closed bud. It reveals the secret of life the sooner.

Bring all the joy you can into your own life, and let it shine elsewhere. Gloom is deadly. The path is upward, the sky is clear, and the sun shines. Remember, the sun shines for all of you. The clouds which lie between are of your own making. One succeeds or fails because of himself, because he has neither the strong desire, the courage, nor the joy of working in his heart. I wish I could make you see what a joy life is. The beauty of it, the swing of it, the life, the song, the color. If you could feel it just once! The raising of your vibrations would dispel all your difficulties, as the sun the fog. You cower before a shadow, the shadow of your own doubt. Get more vibrant with life, and you will sweep everything before you. People will be glad to give you all you want, or need. There is nothing so hypnotic as joy. Get and give all you can. That is our last word for some time. What good is it to you? Try to live out some of the things we suggest and then we may speak again. We greet you and give you God speed.

HELEN AND HARRY

Sister, we must try to explain why Harry developed faster than I did, because there seems to be doubt about it, or rather questioning. Harry arrived here under unusually happy circumstances. I had been preparing for his advent for five years, or from the moment he became a prey to my own deadly disease, T.B. I saw his end from the beginning, and prepared for it by bringing together all who could be made of service towards his rapid development.

You see when I came over there were so few of my own people on my plane that I had but little help, and what development I secured was by my own personal effort, and was of slower acquisition. When one has relatives or friends of such recent arrival here as to be still on the lower planes, one has one's path cleared in advance of stumbling blocks to rapid progress.

Then, too, Harry's mind was far less positive than mine; I mean he was more tolerant of new ideas than I, and more teachable. You will recall that Harry could and did accept correction, even from servants, with a modesty and sense of justice most unusual in a boy or man. No criticism of personal conduct was ever resented by him; he examined each, weighed each, and casting aside the false he accepted the true and just, and acted upon it. This trait is as rare as it is valuable as an asset for rapid development. Harry was always hospitable towards criticism while I blindly resented it.

Over here we have as sharply defined limitations as you have there. One of these was the foreknowledge of the time element in Harry's progress. Latent within his own character lay the strongest instruments of power; modesty, open mindedness and common sense. These were more potent accelerators than even the helping hands of loving relatives.

HELEN

ETERNAL BROTHERHOOD . . .
WE RISE AND FALL
TOGETHER.

20

May 1, 1914
At Evansville, Indiana

ister, we want to say a few words for Papa's birthday. Harry and I will be with you at the factory. Harry is so happy over the way things look there. He is going to be of the party. We both wish the family could see as well as know we are with them. Tell Papa we wish him as few more birthdays there as possible, and a glad welcome here. We can't see when he will come though we have tried hard. We can see that his body here seems quite ready, but we know very little of the laws which release the life spark. Those here who study along these lines are doctors and scientists who have done years of preparatory work on your plane.

There is such a vast field of knowledge to be gained along all lines of work that we all try to specialize. Harry and I belong to the music group. We know that ultimately the paths all converge to a common central point. We detect the gist of things even from here. This common center must be directly the mother of all life as well as all knowledge. The delight of living lies chiefly in the working out of relationships of apparently isolated individual arts or sciences, as well as races and peoples. All are kin; rock and worm; man and angel; all made from the same primeval substance, God or force, no matter what you call it. The father of fire is the mother of water; both come from the same great mysterious beginning. You study there to love your neighbor as yourself. He is yourself, really. You have a hand and a foot, each different, yet each yourself; but neither is all of yourself. You see the drift? When a foot calls a hand an aristocrat and only an ornament, exalting feet as the true useful members, we could smile. One of you is as useful to the whole as the other, and exactly as hard to replace. Each fills his own niche. The mistake is only in the individual point of view, as all life is common to all.

Harry is at the table with you, feel that? I am now talking for him.

Sister, I was touched very deeply at the feeling of the men and all of you. It helps me at my work here to see that after all I was not a complete failure there.[17] What we all need is just to know we haven't had the misfortune to fail utterly in the vital things. I am cut away now from active work at the factory, but see that I can influence the *esprit de corps*.

Yours was a fine idea to increase the beauty of the dining room at the works, as well as the comfort of it. Artistic influences are subtle in their effects on moods and people's feeling. White with[18] "true blue" will be a good foundation. Color has a big significance. Whenever we have time I want to tell what I have learned about color as a factor in soul development.

Dear Mamma! Tell her I sat near her and held her

---

[17] *Harry was General Manager at the Blount Plow Works. The custom for thirty years had been to give a banquet on Mr. Blount's birthday to all the employees and their families. - L.E.B.*

[18] *The name of the best plows. - L.E.B.*

69

hand close in mine. I am glad the flowers were at my place, but that is another story too. What we started to talk about was the absolute kinship of all that exists, things as well as people. When any of us criticize a relative or friend we injure not only ourselves but the whole fabric of life. A selfish or ill-natured thought lowers the rate of vibration of the entire universe, even affecting climate. If people were all unselfish and full of love and real helpfulness there would never be a storm at sea or a railroad wreck. It is the jarring of the rhythmic vibrations all along the line which makes for disaster anywhere. Lightening strikes because someone, somewhere, has violated the law, has had anarchy in his heart. The marvel of this great system is that it takes every atom in it to bring the perfect whole. One atom in rebellion makes for discord all along the line, from earthquake to revolution. Did you ever notice how much more conflict there is in earthquake countries? Did you ever put two and two together? What we can see is that wherever men are inharmonious, earth and climate feel the lack of rhythm, and register the same. All each can do is just to study his own heart and life and see that never for a moment is he in any state but that of love and sympathy toward the rest of the race, as well as toward all other forms of life; from a horse to a rock; from a sky-born star to a tadpole; from a president to a murderer. We are all children of life, linked together close as brain cells. We rise and fall together. No one can rise or fall alone. Never forget that. We belong to the eternal brotherhood of Life. Call it "God" or "Father" if it suits you better. "Life" covers it. There is nothing dead anywhere. The higher one can see, the more humble one grows. Vanity vanishes as the darkness before light when a little knowledge enters.

Oh, you dear ones, don't waste time. Learn this one big truth if you can: "Each for all, and all for each,"[19] because the each *is* the all, and the all is the each. Work for harmony, work for love, work for the united state of all life. There is no escape; no "you" or "I," or "another"; just *all*, necessary parts of God or Life, equal because necessary. Give us the hands of a firmer, sweeter fellowship, we who are here, and you who are there, or seem there. God bless us, every one.

HELEN AND HARRY

---

[19] *This is the motto of the factory. - L.E.B.*

THE SIGNIFICANCE
OF COLORS.

21

June 4, 1914
At Portsmouth, Ohio

elen is here, also Harry. He has been waiting to tell you of several things you might use to advantage. Sister, it is about color as a factor in spiritual advancement. I know you have felt vaguely its influence. That was intuition. That phase of our art study belongs to you. Color has value as it vibrates, either with or against the rhythm of personal harmonics. You see it is allied to music, and to me tone and color are so closely linked I speak of each in terms of the other. Each of us is related through the law of vibration to some tone and color which represents our stage of development. From the lower rates of vibration to the higher there are millions of differences, and as a true progression the soul must pass through each.

The more a soul concentrates the clearer is his or her color. No matter how low in the scale of evolution one is living one should be intensely all that plane indicates. It is the lukewarm attitude which is so deadly. Be all that you feel at this time, but be all of that fearlessly and freely. Get out of each situation all it holds of experience and feeling. Do and be, heartily and sincerely what you feel at the time. If you are on a wrong track the sooner will you reap the harvest of your mistakes and see their error. Then seeing clearly that such and such things cost more than they are worth, you see the point and change accordingly.

Experience alone enables one to graduate from one plane into another. As if we began with fire, say, enjoyed it, felt its warmth, then played with it until it grew and consumed us or what we loved most; then we learned that fire must be governed, controlled, to be of real use to us, and that fire in itself is not at all to be desired or striven for.

When we learn this and raise ourselves to something else, we pass beyond the plane where fire, the passion, and the red, rule. Our own vibratory rate is raised above red, and we have entered the upward path. Red we know and value in its place, and we use it, but we never go after abuse nor let it consume us. Pure, clear red is what no soul can pass by. It is fundamental force. It does things. It is the color of the heart's blood, the inner fire of the earth. No song, no picture, no music can be vital without red and what it represents. It is the dull, muddy shades of red, the passion tinged with selfishness, the fire where sulphurous smoke poisons, the smothering smoke, the dulling, clogging mixtures, which are disheartening to work with. It is never the fearless villain one dreads; it is the sneak, the selfish coward. His personal note is a blur of sound, and his color muddy red. Get him once to be frankly what he is, and there is hope for him.

Colors each have a spiritual or moral meaning. It is the personal law of vibratory rates which gives color a value as an indication of advancement. Each color has as its companion a personal tone which is a harmonic of the color value or note. I find the terms familiar to you hard to use with any real effect. We have an entire vocabulary for this study of musical color.

As we advance we add form as well; then other things whose connection with color seem to you yet more remote. We pass along normal evolutionary lines up the scale of color, each step indicating growth, from simple primary to complex and delicate shadings, ever toward the center and mother of all color which is light: vibrant, palpitating, life-giving light, a single ray of which is blinding to all but perfected souls. You there haven't seen real color or heard one pure musical tone yet. Your nerves couldn't endure it. Whenever a great artist strikes a tone even approaching ours, your hearts melt and you are so emotionally stirred that you are worthless as workers. Fancy how intense life would be with all one's hours filled with such, and far, far better, more thrilling and melting. One must be intense throughout for one's nature to be able to exist in such a tuneful atmosphere.

We are each born with some color and tone dominating us. Harry thinks that to be an indication of a previous life, as each starts at a different point of development. Little John, now, is living in the blue. That is a far more spiritual color than any of us started out with. Harry's note was intense red, a red of power and life. Now he has gone into yellow-orange which indicates spiritualized power. The blue is one of the higher notes, but needs to develop yellow and red to master material success. It is a brain color. Ideas live in it. Harry says it's a "high-brow" color, a fore-runner of the concrete thing men use. Dreams, inventions, books, lie within it, but they are never concrete facts until the soul with that note adds another, either red or yellow, when at once the dream becomes available. As a matter of interest, watch what color next attracts John; green, red, purple, or yellow. He has such keen intuitions you can tell whether it will be power or money he will turn toward. Red, or its mixture, purple, means power or force; green, commercial success.

Sister, we hope we can finish today about the third color, yellow. We were saying yellow is the color of happiness. It is also the color of the life element, the higher life element that strikes you as the sunlight. The sun isn't truly golden, but white; only as it passes along toward you it goes through a sort of reducing process or element which cuts it down to the rate of vibration you can endure.

You see we earth-born souls are pretty low down in the scale of evolution, as you may guess by what you see every day about you. An intelligence so primitive that it must seek personal satisfaction in physical violence or material possessions is very low indeed. It is the infant mind merely, to which such means of satisfaction appeal.

If we have time now let us finish the color story. Yellow is one of the fundamental colors, yet it runs higher even than the blue with you. It has the life element in it. It is the sunlight of vital force toned down from the pure white so as to be endurable to those on our planes. You see we too must live in the light stream. Though we can bear far higher rates of vibrations than you, we still have our limitations of both endurance and perception. There are points beyond which each would lose consciousness. The machinery they carry would fail to register anything. Only the gradual growth of all one's senses enables one to see and hear and feel what transpires about us when on an elevation above our normal or present one.

Enfolded within each is the germ of everything, the capacity to become. It is no greater miracle than the oak within the acorn. It takes certain exterior agents or conditions to develop the oak, just as it does to develop higher perceptions. Light exists, life exists over, through, and about us. But we perceive it only gradually. The life without calls to itself within, and then petal by petal, idea by idea, the flower and the man's heart open.

Life, love, light! It's all one. It is always calling to its enclosed self to come forth and complete its functioning on that plane, that it may make the circle of life again higher. The yellow represents the joy of living, of motion, of doing. It is the symbol of happiness, as red is of force, and blue of mind.

HELEN

75

BUILDING
SPIRITUAL
BODIES.

22

June 25, 1914
At Portsmouth, Ohio

ister: We wish to send a message to the folks for the wedding dinner.[20] Harry and I want to tell them how much we wish they could see us when they are all at the table. We shall be with them, bringing the light of the upper country where Harry is now living, and where I work a great deal. We can take your spirit there too if you will sit alone at the dinner hour.

Papa has been coming over here almost every day, and we can see his face so clearly, as it will be when he is all here. Mamma has been building her body too, much more rapidly than Papa, in the last few weeks. We wonder if she won't be ready to come here as soon as, or even before, Papa does. I feel she must do all she has to do without any waste of time. Her body is far more beautiful than it was six months ago. She must realize that time to work there is short, and so she can't afford any but fine

---

[20] *A celebration of the Golden Wedding of the parents was participated in by all the children except "Sister" and her husband, who could not be present. For the convenience of children living at a distance the celebration was not held on the exact anniversary day. - L.E.B.*

thoughts and happy days. We feel it most fitting, the reunion coming now, and on your birthday too. You could be better spared than any of the others, as we represent you there, and you have already given all you could to increase the harmony in the family. The absence of a person's body is a little thing when his spirit is right. We shall be with you in the morning, and at home with the family in the afternoon. We will give a birthday letter. You have been doing well.

HELEN

THE HIGHEST JOY:
GIVING UP
OF SELF.

23

June 26, 1914
At Portsmouth, Ohio

One's path in any race must be cleared for action if there is to be distance travelled. One may gain for soul advancement under trying conditions, but work for the public must be done under smooth, easy, personal surroundings. One has more energy left for the race if one has not to stop and mend the road. There is always need of workers for the general or public good, and to make these most effective we try to clear their path of stumbling blocks.

Here we are always looking for people to serve the masses. When one is found with a show of promise for such work, we try him out to see how much strain he can bear, and then lead him to the gaps which need filling, and his intuition forces him into the public service.

National life must be maintained by the voluntary service of the strong, who set aside their smaller personal problems for the sake of public duty. Hopeful timber is being selected constantly by those who work here. The possible saviours are being sorted out and put into training to leaven the mass of slow moving humanity. They are tested out in a hundred ways for the role of some impending service. A weakling, at the point of greatest strain in a crisis, retards the evolution of an entire race sometimes. We here also must make no mistakes.

When any souls on your plane can sink their personal ambition or vanity in love for the rest of the race, they then become candidates for the class of higher service, and we make their personal path as easy and free as possible. When one can be willing to lose his life for others he then saves it for himself. It is like learning to swim. When you relax and stop struggling you float. All the big things follow the same law. The wild desire for self-preservation kills, because the mind is not relaxed nor receptive, and the flow of knowledge is cut off. No one generates knowledge by himself. He is just a medium for the expression of existing truth. The less he thinks he is, or knows, the more he can express. Your mind can obstruct or discolor the light, but it does not create it. It is merely a transmitter. You see the point?

There is a succession of graduated planes or evolutionary steps over here, each governed or mastered by the most advanced soul on that plane, who is responsible for the work in that division. Above him are others, ever higher, ever more complex or exalted. The great general plan is doubtless known only to the Ultimate Mind or Creator, each lower master working out some idea or detail, which in its turn fits in with some other part.

The same plans descend to you. No one man on earth knows the entire plan of the earth's solution. He does his small part, and should be proud to do it well for the beauty of the ultimate product. We deal only with the transient details. We waste little time speculating on failures. We are too busy. We revel in the splendid swing of life as it is in the making, and gladly do our part. The greater our capacity and intelligence, the more we see to do and be. The one who can does freely and without stint. There is neither the desire nor the idea of holding back. We throw all we have, and are, into the stream, and find our highest joy in giving up self.

It is hard to get any real true idea of the plan of

life over to you, but perhaps it is not a waste of energy to try at least. You and Tee have responded so well thus far that it is a great happiness to us here, and our vision of what you may be able to do expands. The limit lies with your own mental attitude merely. So long as you are in a receptive state you will grow. When your minds close we are helpless to serve you except in the slightest way, at points you have left, as it were, unlocked.

HELEN

HOW TO CREATE CONDITIONS TO RECEIVE SPIRITUAL LOVE.

24

July 5, 1914
At Portsmouth, Ohio

es, Sister, we are here. Harry is always with me, as a matter of course. You need have no fear of his being away at any time. It has been in our minds to ask you to let us work out one of our questions of personality, and its force or power over different people, through either you or Tee as mediums of transmission. We have been able, so far, to get over several ideas to each of you. Now suppose we try to work out our theory of personal power, or the omnipotence of the creative element of love. Let either of you put all your surplus energy into a desire, say, for a larger field of work. As it happens, your work lies at present along parallel lines, so what either desires means better conditions for both. Put your combined forces therefore into the same channel. Both desire a winter of broader use and fullness, with a higher position for Tee, and a broader acquaintance for you. Back of personal desire must lie altruistic motive in order to attract and hold the helpers here. Let your hearts fill with love and sympathy for your fellows; expect help from us; than ask for a larger place to work. The details as to how and where will be our business. We are unhampered by physical limitations, and can find what we seek for better than you. The push which brings you into the bigger stream of life

81

will be the elemental or fundamental desire to help. Trust us for details, and don't waste energy in worry or disintegrating emotions of any sort. Keep as happy as possible. Let the spirit of tolerance and charity tinge every thought you entertain toward anyone. This is absolutely essential to any successful help from us. We cannot work where vibrations are discordant.

The master says if Tee will habituate himself to working by day he can master his parts quicker. Night work is bad because of the drain to which a preoccupied mind is open from vampire souls who are strongest at night. In sleep we are with him, but we cannot help him when he studies at night instead of sleeping. Repair work should be done at night by his body plus our force, but conditions are not good during daylight for repair, as life is active and we are going against the current. Hughey says to try sleeping at night for two weeks, and see if it will not improve his work. He can study out of doors if he likes by day, and he will discover that his memory will improve under altered conditions. Let him take the car and go out early and sit by some stream and study an hour or two alone. His brother will be beside him. Let him try it for two weeks, as a test of what day work and night sleep will do, and let him watch both his bodily and mental vigor.

> *Au revoir,*
> *HELEN, HARRY and always*
> *HUGHEY, too, we three*

You were right about special direction as to work. . . . .It is a plan in process of construction. You are particularly responsive to the ideas we discuss. Harry laughs over it, saying: "Watch Sister catch that." It is this response which makes you appear to originate ideas. This is a blow, Sister, but never mind. It is fine to be a true transmitter. All ideas come from above. They have to filter some distance before even we get them. Oh, we do not mean that every detail of your life is filtered down to you. It is only the big ideas. Any of us can crystallize a detail from the main mass. Only, as Harry says, by the time you get it most of the combinations have been worked. Harry's sense of humor is always alive and busy.

HELEN

LOVE, SERVE . . .
ESCAPING THE LOWER
SOUL ELEMENT.

25

July 14, 1914
At Portsmouth, Ohio

ister, we do want to tell you something new. Your depression is due entirely to the currents of trouble in and about your house. There are several people near you whom you have attracted, a large number of souls from the dark countries, where even we rarely go except under guards who can lift us quickly at any dangerous sign. Neither you nor we have the resistance to cope with a number of these darker souls. Now, it was this truth about the law we wished you to know. You yourself belong to the brighter country in the yellow light, and so at all normal times you are buoyant, cheerful. Whenever you get "low in your mind," as you say, it is always the result of a depressant from without, and at such times you should go away somewhere and stay for hours. You would be better at the park, or out of town as many hours a day as possible. That is why the motor is so needful to you three. Keep one always, no matter where you go, as an escape from what cities are frequently so full of: that is, the lower soul element from here. It is not the landlady's troubles so much that depress you. It is the disembodied trouble you cannot see. Being such a good transmitter you feel the bad as well as the good, and need this warning.

Why can't we protect you? Because we need our force for constructive work, not just to act as life preservers or shields for you. Were this to be any permanent injury we should of course guard you at all points, but it isn't so serious, so we just decided to warn you and let you care for yourself.

We are at work on your winter's location now. You will be well cared for then, and can go away in April at the latest. Tee should get a full three months on the other side, Harry and his brothers say. John won't be in the way, Sister. He is part of our plan.

I see you feel somewhat peevish at being only the instrument of our plans, but you are mighty important to us, as well as to the two you and we wish to serve and develop for higher service. Remember your motto is "Love, Serve." You don't wish to lead or shine really, Sister, down in your heart. Your motto is a true one. It is a big and beautiful thing to serve with love. It is the song of the golden country where your home will be, so never despise any service, however low, for any you love. To gain your permanent residence in that country you must serve those whom you despise, with love. That is the deed that opens the gates there. To serve the mean, the selfish, the vicious with a patience and an overwhelming love. What you do is easy, sweet, and full of rewards, as your journey takes you nearer the place you seek. The love must be so big, so fine, and so strong that it can blot out all the others' mean unworthiness, and leave only pity. They know not what they do, but you know that for you, now and always, the motto is "Love, Serve." Now go, and you three hunt up a new road. Never mind mud. Get out and away. We all ask it.

It is all right about Tee's work. He will find the right thing soon, so do not let worry enter in at all. We are with you in force now, and can protect you all three from evil influences, so be at peace. That is the attitude needed for results. No need to write more. You do well to read over our letters often. It augments the connection between us. Be of good cheer; all is going well.

ALL THREE H'S

VITAL FORCE . . . MAGNETISM, DRAIN, AND REST.

26

July 21, 1914
At Portsmouth, Ohio

Yes, Sister, it is I, Helen. We are so glad John is safe from the illness he was drifting toward. Don't get discouraged about being nervous. We have been getting so much vitality from you for both the others that you are a bit short yourself. You will be balanced again soon. We will help you. You see we can fill your vital tank, as it were, so easily. We get a bit careless sometimes, and let your reserve fall too low. When you began sneezing yesterday we saw it and made provisions for you. When any of you get cold and shiver, the vital force has gone below the point where it is safe. . . .Never mind, it is not a bad interruption. What I want to say is that you must get away early and alone with Tee tonight. You need the rest and quiet to get your equilibrium. You will be rested to-morrow. We think you had better not take any more long drives in a party. Go alone, you three. You and John need more space to rest in. It would have been better all around had you gone alone Sunday. Never take so many so far again. They are like vampires when they get tired, and the most sensitive get drawn on to supply the lack. The car might carry four, if the fourth were quiet and congenial; but never five, for over an hour's trip. After about an hour they will begin to vampirize

87

you. Remember, in Harry's last drive how tired Marie was? Harry used all her vitality, and took so much of it he lasted hours longer than he could otherwise have done. Of course this absorption of another's vital force or magnetism is unconscious, and so none can be blamed for being the vampire. We tell you as a warning. Don't let anyone go with you abroad, either, no matter how much they may want to go. Only you three are in our plan. It is all we can work for this time.

HELEN

FOCUS YOUR WILL
WITH A GLAD HEART . . .
FORM IS TRANSIENT, MIND IS SUBSTANCE. 27

July 27, 1914
Portsmouth, Ohio

Note: Before communication was thoroughly established between Sister and Helen a meaningless jumble of words from some outside influence was crowded in.
L.E.B.

ister, why will you allow that? We told you yesterday we would not write again, but we knew you were too weak to resist these people who have been trying so long to get closer to you as a good way to vitalize themselves. Harry wouldn't leave you till we had made our warning stronger. Tee is also being experimented with from this side. Tell him, for all our sakes, to put a watch on his own soul when asleep. His will can protect him if he sets his mind to pray, as a small child, for safety while asleep. He was taken to see the lower souls whose desires have misshapen their spiritual bodies. Such visits weaken him. He must not allow them. Let him call on Hughey when he is in trouble, or let the love of his own heart

89

blaze up and shield him. His enemy was one of the advocates of greed, hate, and power of a low order. In all spiritual encounters Love is the conquering weapon; Love and Pity.

We would have told you all about our work yesterday, only you were all in, as Harry says, and we stopped earlier than we had expected. We have been doing constructive work for the raising of color and sounds into shapes similar to buildings, bridges, and tunnels; a sort of combination architecture and engineering work. Every material expression in life is the visible form of some mental quality or attribute. Bridges represent the extending of a helping hand to a fellow in need. Tunnels burrow deep through some problem of life, seemingly insurmountable. It is one way out or through a difficulty. There is always a way to arrive over, under, or through. One just *must* arrive. One with spiritual material can master and transmute ideas or things into many expressed forms.

The will is back of all effort. Then we take our closer medium of expression and push through that to other forms or construction. You see one can change the medium of expression (as that horrid soul did his form) without at all weakening what is behind it. Form, or the apparently solid thing, is actually fluidic, transient. Mind, Spirit, Idea, Motive, is the true substance. Circumstance never really hampers anyone. As we have explained repeatedly, it is the indestructible thing behind it. Call it God, Will, Mind, Personality, what you please. Spirit is as good a term as we need. To be able to project one's spirit into a given channel for a definite purpose, and hold it there against the opposing current until it fulfills its purpose: this is to cultivate power as belongs to the infinite; to feel steadily, to be, and do, one thing, then turn and do one other thing with the same steadfastness and concentration. You can begin this practice, carefully making plans, then focussing your will and thought upon them till they materialize before you. Harry says the trick has been turned by all masters of finance. They simply knew what they wanted, and bent iron wills to that one end.

Any quality grows by what it feeds upon. Power upon power, greed upon greed, until one gets into the higher law, when one gains by giving up. One grows strong by yielding. One conquers by love, never by hate. This is the thing we call the law. Whenever we refer to "law" we mean the rule of the spirit, or the life-giving, dominating quality called love in all its phases.

If Tee in his struggles last night had simply stood still and turned on his tormentors the full force of his power of love, there would have been a revelation he might live years before realizing. Let him think and feel more about this truth, about what Hughey has demonstrated, and the thing Hughey showed him.

Our work goes deeper and ever deeper into its marvelous power. As we work we grow, and, growing, wish for you and that you could learn this principle before you come here. Not for your own sake, because you could learn it here as we did, but for what that knowledge would do for others there; people we cannot reach except indirectly. Personal contact means so much to the undeveloped soul, still groping hopelessly for some solid footing for the will to stand upon; some sure feeling as a starting point from which to fight the hidden enemies. Personal contact is a great thing.

Tee must live and develop for the sake of his weaker associates in the theater. They need what he is able to give. He should give more to all in and about the place where he works. Let him take personal interest in all at the theaters, and say the right word to help. Let them see that he cares whether they go up or down. Let him be more of a . . . yes, Sister, write what is in your head . . . "buttinsky." That's it. Let him take an interest and talk more. Remember, we are none of us here for ourselves, but for the sake of every human being whose life touches ours. Every one of them is a part of our business here. We leave none without some mark upon them of our making, for better or for worse. We pass this way but once. This is our great opportunity. Look to it that we all do our very best every day, to each and every human heart our spirit touches. Let us leave a trail of blessing in our wake. Selfishness isn't always aggressive. Sometimes it is most active when we shut ourselves away, when we think we are minding our own business best. It is then we are idlest, most selfish. People are our business. Better be a spendthrift than a miser, any day. Give to all who need the little word of warning or encouragement. Love is in the open with a glad heart, and the sun will shine on you as well as on those you try to help.

We feel it is time to go now, Sister. Don't try to write. If you find you need help we will come, but not unless it is necessary. You must leave off long enough to let those other people who use you stop trying. We have really given you all you need. Be content. Protect yourself from invasion, and blessings will follow you. Our love is always about you.

**HELEN, HARRY, and
the MASTER**

THERE MUST BE A PLAN,
A VISION . . .
BEFORE ANYTHING CAN MATERIALIZE.

28

July 28, 1914
At Portsmouth, Ohio

ll right, Sister. We are here and have come to tell you about our work on a still higher plane. We shall be vibrating at a vastly greater rate. Helen will be nearer you, but she feels you cannot stand such frequent drains on your nerve force. No, we shall be nearer you than before, in one way, but at the same time less able to let you hear from us directly, so we wish you to take what we have previously given and know that the future will be looked after, and that Tee will be helped always if he is cheerful; and particularly if he is hopeful, that being a state of mind easier to lift higher. This he knows already. Plan for the trip abroad of which we spoke. Use every means present-ed for advancement along all lines or branches of Tee's work. If he will let himself dream dreams and build castles as you do, they will be more apt to materialize than if he is simply patient and waits for circumstances to open the way. Make plans, look forward joyfully to good times, and you will then be well on your way there. The planning of futures is not an empty pastime; it is the building plans, the blueprint of the work. Nothing just happens. Someone's mind first makes the blueprint, then all can help to construct the thing into visible form. Sister's long suit is dreaming dreams. Tee's hopelessness about his own future cut off that future but for the force of Sister's optimism. If Tee will look back he will trace all sorts of things to Sister's visions. Her plans so often come true because she made them. Had he made them they would have come just as swiftly. It is not the person; it is the law. There must be a plan, a vision, what you will, before anything can materialize for either good or bad. The law works both ways. Make plans; think of them; see them coming; and those of us here who love you most will build in all the parts beyond your reach.

Tee has so far taken our suggestions so well we feel this one last step will put him into the independent class. Let him think out just what he wants, then expect to get it, and go after it without doubt in his heart, and it is his.

A mastering ambition or desire carries all before it. Apparent obstructions crumble at its confident approach and melt away. Nothing can withstand the determined march of the spirit toward its own. You can't ever fail because of outside obstacles. The real and only obstacles lie within yourself. Never forget that, either of you. Make definite plans and see how easily material things obey the command of the soul.

Re-read all we have said from time to time, and speed gladly on your own way. With love in your hearts, and joy in your eyes, nothing can down you. We shall be near, working and watching and loving.

The master says he may teach again by a dream if need be, but not for long, he thinks. Don't feel us far. The better you know the law the closer we will be drawn. Time is nothing. We shall soon meet for work, and study, and larger service.

Au revoir,

HELEN, HARRY
and HUGHEY

THE WAR (W.W.I) . . .
WITHOUT FRIENDSHIP,
NONE EVER REALLY CONQUERS.

29

August 26, 1914
At New York City

The War, you know, is only a faint reflection of the real conflict here, where elements can be wielded with a force appalling to us who are still among the non-combatants. You see, here we are having the long deferred struggle which seems to occur at stated intervals in the history of the world's evolution.

Now and again there seem to evolve two separate forces here which appear to be in direct opposition. What generates the darker half or evil of life we cannot tell from where we look on. In the larger plan of life it must be only a logical part of the human or soul's evolution. Our vision here is too limited to see the causes or larger plan, which makes these occasional titanic struggles necessary and right, or at least, only a phase of the normal action and reaction of life forces.

To us, here where we can see, a seething mass of souls desperately struggling for seeming existence, it is difficult to keep our mental poise and realize that there is nothing but good, which always conquers. This lesson has been taught us from a hundred different angles, that it might enter and arouse our minds against all sorts of apparent conflicting facts, and in order that we should always believe so firmly in the power of good as to be, in a way, impregnable

95

to any contrary idea.

The vast, world-wide struggle is a part of the plan of evolution. In the processes of all growth there are always generated elements or forces which when occurring in larger quantities than necessary, must be eliminated from the body of matter, as is true in your physical bodies. You generate in the processes of digestion, for instance, certain acids and gases which are essential to the manufacture of blood and bodily tissue. When these products are manufactured in excess there is a general disturbance all through the system, necessitating drastic measures for the prevention of destructive results. Then some disagreeable but quite necessary acute disease ensues, and destroys the superabundant poisonous acids, and an equilibrium is restored.

We feel that law is consistent and holds good all along the line, and all we need to understand it is to observe its working carefully at any minor point. Force is a most necessary element in progressive evolution, yet force carries with it certain destructive elements such as the selfish lust of power which is born of arrogance, which is also a child of ability or capacity. When any soul has the capacity to achieve, he also has the latent desire to rule, to dominate. The greatest thing we can conceive is a soul which has capacity for achievement, and with it humility, sympathy, and love. This seems to be the mark of the perfected human soul. One must have force and individual capacity, or there is no forward movement; but force must learn that even it yields to the higher law. "The meek shall inherit the earth," because with the pride of power goes the element of self-destruction.

Watch your view of war. Germany has the force and the arrogance. She must learn the subsequent lesson of humility and service. Force is blind and so can only be taught by the means it can comprehend. We feel there is now enough unselfish love on earth to save the weak from annihilation. Up here we join all our forces to strengthen the line of opposing love. We have no doubts as to the ultimate issue. Hughey has gone to throw all he possesses of light into the dark struggle, caused by ignorance, he thinks. Where the light shines, the truth can be perceived and the struggle ceases. Love and intelligence are one. No one breaks the Law who realizes the futility of such an act. When anyone or any nation fails to realize the common brotherhood of nations he is ignorant of the Law, and so liable to the penalty.

We rise or fall as a common whole, not in isolated groups. Each, by his habitual thought, allies himself with either the lifters, or the drags. See to it that you guard carefully your every thought, that you may do your part in the enlightening of the world. The Law acts with you as with us. Tee and you both must absolutely eliminate all destructive ideas and emotions for the good of the whole, incidentally only for your own. The chain is just as strong as its weakest link. You and he are both links, and upon each depends far more than any realize. Live your own lives well because this living (and by this living I mean mental life as well) affects all other souls, both below and above. If the integrity of a single atom can affect a universe then imagine what damage a selfish, disordered, gloomy mind can do. We belong to the brotherhood of man. Let us be sure we can qualify for that fraternity.

Conflict such as is raging now is terrible, but hopeful too, for it means a purifying of the body of the earth; a fresh start on a higher plane. The surplus force and the destructive energy will spend itself. Then what remains will have learned a great lesson, viz.: the futility of struggle and the hopelessness of trying to conquer by force. The Germans never really conquered France. To do that they should have shown brotherly love and sympathy, as we did to the Southern army when conquered. Without friendship, without sympathy, none ever really conquers. Will the conquerors now learn that? Will they rejoice at another's increase in trade, in art, or in science? Will they really learn to be brothers? We shall see. This is the real issue: the conquering of jealousy and selfish greed. All must learn to live and let live. We call on all to do their part. Let us belong to the glad volunteers, giving our best freely and fully. Our best in this case is a steadfast optimism in the good on all planes of life. Faith in all that lifts the mass of ignorant life, faith in our own share of that work, belief in our ability to master material conditions, to do our work in the best way. Faith, not in ourselves as geniuses, but as fit instruments for human betterment.

HELEN

HOW TO
QUALIFY FOR
IMMORTALITY.

30

September 24, 1914

his will be a straight dictation from Harry, so, as the "middleman," I, Helen, shall obliterate myself; this being Harry's day. . .

Greetings for you all on this birthday of mine. While I have grown vastly and complexly in certain directions in this year of your time, I am at heart just as I was at parting, full of the personal interests of each and all. We, who have lived and worked on this side of life for any space of time, realize that family association means very little as regards the age question or the physical relationship of parent and child, brother and sister. We know that ties, based upon mutual understanding, link with far stronger bonds than mere blood connection. What any two have in common, whether it be work or aspiration, is the "tie that binds." It so easily becomes natural to drop into comradeships here, with either young or old, men or women, when there is a common interest. There is no age which demands respect or reverence. Only the merit of a strong and beautiful character can receive either. Conventional standards are non-existent. The spirit, being of a stability you little comprehend, sets its own standard, and those who pass into this life must perforce accept this standard. One has no choice any more than one has about mathematics, as two and two

99

being four is past argument at all times and in every place. It is so here about the attributes of character. A selfish act is a selfish act in all places, and in all epochs of time. For such there is always but one opinion. There are no such things as extenuating circumstances. First, of course, one must define one's terms. A selfish act is a simple proposition. Anything which does not consider the personal consequences to the *other fellow first* is selfish. A spoken word which has the power to wound another, no matter how carelessly dropped into the air, has weight in the final judgment. No soul has a right, consciously or unconsciously, to lay burdens on any other. It may be that this other is just struggling to lift its head out of the dark pool of ignorance, straining every nerve to drag its heavy body up into the light; it quivers with the strain of effort. At this point a careless push, however light, may plunge it backward from whence it came, retarding its evolution for years, perhaps for ages.

We are brothers all, and the soul's development is a result of what the strong do for the weak. Chivalry abhors the coward who strikes a cripple, a child, or a woman, but what sort of human is it who refuses his hand to a brother because of that brother's ignorance, dirt, or color? There are no terms black enough for the sins of the spirit. Intolerance, contempt, repulsion: these belong to cowards. These are what retard evolution, not war or bloodshed. The darkest crimes are bloodless. The deepest sin is not in your criminal code. You fail even to recognize it as such. This much I have learned of the true law since I came. Brotherhood, in its deepest meaning, is the comprehensive term. It is not so much food and money the poor need, but love and a true, not a patronizing sympathy.

What are we, half . . . yes, even less than half . . . developed humans that we are? We know nothing of true values. We smile at the savage who barters priceless ivory for a piece of red calico, or a bit of mirror, but we give all that is finest in us, crush all that is best in others, for money or power. We barter eternal soul-stuff in return for transient gain, which, even as we clutch at it, melts away. Our bonds prove worthless, our big palaces burn down, our art treasures are stolen or cut to pieces. The savage has made an even trade. His gold and ivory were only material, as was that he received in return. His soul was no poorer after the exchange than before. He lived wisely, but any man who values money, or its equivalent, above the spiritual thing he usually loses to attain it, is in truth the ignoramus, to use the mildest of terms. A man outwits his competitor, gains what his brother loses, and counts himself honest. It is not honest to use one's superior wisdom to rob a child, even though the child make no out-cry.

We *are* our brother's keeper. His ultimate good should be our first thought and our last. True charity teaches the man to help himself, and it goes deeper than material limitations. The rich, that is the wise, are the protectors of the poor, the ignorant. The wise man must have the loving patience of the true mother to really be worth an immortal soul and a continuous life.

Our work here is on a far higher plane than yours, and so it is with a sort of misgiving I shall attempt explanation. We work with the living matter you call emotions or impulses, which rise spontaneously from the love or devotion of some person or thing. It is handled as one of you handles and works with and upon an electric current. We take some given emotion, follow it back until we find its source or root, then classify it and take another.

Emotions and motives lie deep in the secret places of each soul, and are the fibers of which character is made. When any soul has enough of the vital emotions, of worthy and unselfish motives in him, to be twisted into a thread of strength, he is then sure of protracted evolution. This thread or cable is what anchors him, or rescues him from shipwreck as he journeys from life to life, across the sea of death

101

and rebirth. I fear I have no simile apt enough to explain the idea. We speak a differing language.

The whole thing resolves itself into the vital question of how much eternal stuff any one soul possesses to live on indefinitely. We dissect a character as a student at a medical school dissects a body. We find that when a nature has selfishness developed beyond a given point he disintegrates. But one, no matter how heavily laden with defects other than that, evolves if he only has love of his kind strong within him.

Love, or active sympathy with one's human fellow, seems to be the strongest fiber known. It passes all sorts of tests with absolutely indestructible quality, whereupon we conclude that this then is vitally important tq man's individual progress. No true thing is lost, but individuality is something one achieves and keeps only because one has at the bottom true love and sympathy for one's neighbor. To love one's neighbor as oneself is simply the law of self preservation, and I might add that if you don't do that your game ends right there.

"Them that has, gets." Yes, and those who have not the love referred to are promptly relieved of whatever qualities they have that are worth while. These can be taken and appropriated by any who have the vital spark which only insures continuous individual existence.

It is as if a chair should lack a seat, thus becoming absolutely worthless for the purpose for which it was created. The chair may have an excellent back and several perfect legs, but these avail nothing when a chair is seatless, though they may be used to beautify or strengthen some other chair, and always do this service, as nothing good can be lost. You see that, don't you?

The vital part of an individual is his heart, his love. Take that away and his game is up. His hair and teeth and bones can be useful elsewhere, but they serve another individual. The "I," the particular ego that heart made, is non-existent. He couldn't qualify. So it behooves all and each of you to regard carefully your main asset. Add to it continuously to prevent a final dissolution. No one can afford to take chances, or rest on his oars. Neither you nor I know what tests of character lie ahead. We are in the stream of evolution. Those weaklings who fail to meet its tests perish. The tests are varied and constant, and unperceived until passed. One must prepare constantly for the day of reckoning. None of us are ever quite ready for the test, and we escape by a hair's breadth only. One can't dodge. The progress of the stream is slow but steady, and we must work continuously to survive.

Look into your own hearts and note your wares. Try out each thing you see there. See if it has real value, is made of eternal stuff. Get a line on true values, what in life is of vital importance. The test is always:

Can you take the thing with you out of life?

A hasty glance seems to show that one can take nothing. Look again. One takes patience, charity, unselfishness, another's gratitude, which is blessing, too. One may take the result of kindness and help which expanded and lifted another human pilgrim. Sunshine, courage, simple faith, and sweetness. Oh! the things we may carry away are manifold. The man or woman who lays aside a business problem to care for the distress or perplexity of a little child has chosen the real and laid by the unimportant thing. Any help to a soul in trouble is a vital service which registers here, and helps determine what class you enter.

While time doesn't exist here, opportunity and work do, and progression is continuous, so I feel that for the good of all you should waste no time. Do what you may while you have the chance. People whose needs you can supply move on, out of your circle, and your chance to help and to grow go with them. No day passes without an opportunity. It's sickening to see how many you let slip. Why not try to live a day at a time? One can only chew what he has in his mouth. What remains on his plate doesn't concern him.

If you would all do this; concentrate on the day's work, keeping eyes wide open to see a brother's need! Oh, it makes my heart swell to think what that would mean. Today is really all you have for service, for growth; yet you sit idle, with busy hands and empty hearts. You sit and play with toys while your brother is drowning within your arm's reach. With vacant eyes fixed on some selfish golden future you sit. Strong men and women, you sit inactive, letting your chance of immortality slip past you.

Wake up. Rouse yourself. Be worth immortality. Earn it. This bloody war typifies what you all are, in less degree. Which of you is entitled to cast the first stone? Which of you but has wounded some heart, trodden on some upturned face seeking only the light?

Ignorance is no excuse. The Law holds all to account. When any of you can show love, pity, and sympathy for each human soul you meet, then, and only then have you the right to cast the first stone. Live the good your heads know, try to qualify for immortality. Speak less and do more.

But I see I write too long. Forgive the sting if there be any in these last lines. I love you all too deeply to speak but for your help. We must lay aside smaller interests for greater. A glad, warm hand-clasp I give you this day.

HARRY (through Helen)

WE GENERATE
OUR OWN LIGHT.

31

October 23, 1914
At Orangeburg, South Carolina

es, now we are all three here. Oh, not at all, a dull place, Sister. It's quite radiant if you could but see, really. It's as the "Living Dead Man"[21] said: "We generate our own light here, and so it is always just as bright as we are within," which naturally varies with each individual, but when several of us unite we make any room gay.

It's first to discuss the Western trip.

The master says he will arrange things as well as possible. He likes the idea, because it means so much for his mother. He feels if he can bring pleasure to her before she comes over here she can live better here. Her life lacks the happy elements, and she worries so much she is enveloped in a cloud most of the time. Tee is her brightest light, and he can do her more good than anyone there, with the exception of the grandchildren, John especially. Hughey wishes her to see more of you and John, as well as Tee. To this end we will all work. But remember, the plan must be made by you and Tee, and we will fill in only the parts you can't manage yourselves.

---

[21] *A book, "Letters from a Living Dead Man",*
written down by Elsa Barker.

Harry and I will go with you as our holiday, and I believe Harry will enjoy it as much as you can. He so loved a camp, especially sleeping out under the stars. You have a few pleasures we can't have here. That's why Harry insists we reincarnate. There is a zest and charm about a rough camp and a red fire with smoke in your eyes, and burned meat, which beats any meal civilization can get up. Harry says he is sure the lure of the flesh, and what that means in the hand to hand grapple with material conditions, will draw him back to rebirth, but not yet. He must know more of this place, and work out some things with you and Tee before you return in a group to rebirth and work on earthly planes again.

The book[22] you are reading has fired Harry, and he and the master both determined to prove what is there stated. Even Hughey hasn't been about as much as he might, because of his work and service; but at this time, as a reaction after the war struggle, he will travel and study more, serving less for a time.

Harry has found a company now who claim they can show him a soul reincarnate. With this proof before us, we shall, for a time at least, stop our creative work and try to find our past lives, and by the trend of these see what we lack most, and readjust our work accordingly. We never knew until last night when you read it, that we both, with Hughey's help, might have built a protecting wall about you so those evil souls couldn't have disturbed you. Now, however, you have protected yourself, so perhaps it is just as well.

There is so much to learn, and we love it all. Harry says he was getting too much absorbed in the marvels of the law to follow up other threads. We all feel that we have learned enough of the Law of Love and Brotherhood to have it become a part of ourselves, so we may follow other lines of knowledge now.

---

[22] *"Letters from a Living Dead Man."*

You can see now that the new ideas don't all come from us; that you can teach us as well as we you. It's a mutual exchange of benefits.

HELEN

QUESTS FOR INFORMATION.

32

At Florence, South Carolina

Yes, Sister, Helen. I can write if you wish it this evening, but prefer daylight. Yes, Harry and I sat with you on the bed and listened to that book. He is going to hunt up that man, and get more data on reincarnation. He knows several masters who teach other things, mostly science along medical lines, but he hasn't been off alone yet on any separate quests for information.

Can't Tee read us some more before dinner? Thanks. We are all ears.

HELEN

THE DEAD ARE NO MORE HOLY
THAN THEY WERE
BEFORE THEY DIED.

33

October 30,1914

am here Sister, Helen. What do you think we had better do about the preface to the book of our letters?

Harry says you really needn't write it at all. He thinks as the letters are for private circulation only, what need of the conventional preface? Besides Bess wouldn't care for those first letters, anyway. Both she and Rose are easily shocked, and Harry's letters written just after coming here have a strong earthly flavor. They are in fact, decidedly human. To some this fact is additional proof of the individual existence after bodily dissolution. Again, however, those strictly masculine passages shock the sense of decorum. They seem, in a way, sacrilegious. The so-called dead are in reality no more holy than they were before they died; but on the other hand custom has built up a sort of sanctified atmosphere about those passed beyond, which it may not be worth while to disturb. It's another of the beautiful Santa Claus myths which hurt no one.

So as Sister suggests suppose you print the letters as leaflets; then use discrimination in their distribution. Let them stand on their merits, without any word of comment or explanation.23

Yes, Sister, we didn't wish you to stay longer because of what Mamma was doing. You can help her with her giving away her things. Tell her to give as many things outright as she can. It will all help to lighten her own craft, and she can do far higher work there as soon as she has fewer possessions about her. Let her keep what lace and jewelry she can and will wear herself. Only a few choice things she can keep. Let her decide what, and where the things are to go, and then ship them out of the house. This alone will raise her vibrations to great extent. Simplify life. Cut down the clothing as low as her best judgment counsels. Let her keep no more about her than she could travel with in two trunks.

We wanted you to help her do this. You had better send the pink dress to Bess.24 You won't wear it. Send away to her what you see you won't wear this winter. Lace and a few good bits of jewelry you can use, and these won't hurt your progress. Everything else should be wisely passed on. Cut down! Cut down! And then again, cut down!

We see a great work ahead for you and Mamma, so we want you both cleared for action.

HELEN

---

23 *This in reference to the pamphlet in which some of these letters were first printed for private circulation. - L.E.B.*

24 *A sister.*

THE GIFT OF AN ABLE TRANSMITTER . . 34
AND MORE ABOUT HARPIES
AND VAMPIRES.

November 1, 1914

ister: Several of us wish to write today, so plan to stay at home. Perhaps I had better write first, as I'll tire you least of anyone. What you wished to know was why I didn't write for over twenty years. Two reasons: first, because it was bad for you; and second, because I was being trained for service.

When anyone on your plane has the gift you have of being an able transmitter, or a true medium of communication between the two worlds of earth and spirit, they are, by that quality, a target or focus for all those who live upon the earth on human magnetism. Those vampires (for such they become if allowed) have the power to draw off all the surplus vitality of one on your plane, till that one has no reserve left with which to combat disease should he fall a victim to that.

Worse, these harpies from our side have neither judgment nor mercy, and they often take not only their victim's surplus, but what he needs to live upon from day to day, reducing him to a physical as well as a mental wreck. This I learned soon after coming here, and so, not because I lost interest, but as a matter of safeguarding you, I kept away.

I learned that there are safe means of communication open to those whose vibratory rate is high enough to take them above the lowest plane where

111

the vicious live. So, never doubting that sooner or later we would resume our lost connection, I did my part to raise myself above the danger zone.

Harry has spoken often of how strange it was that you held me so faithfully in your thoughts all these years, as if I were as vital a personality as when I left. I was often with you, especially down in Cuba, and before John came. Harry is sure it indicates a far older and stronger tie in some mental past shared together, loving and loved. Perhaps he is right; I can't say. I prefer proof to surmise. When I see a soul incarnate itself I shall know. Meantime I listen. It is quite possible such a place exists, as this universe is so vast it would take centuries to see it all, and seeing, to understand.

I am one who works and waits for my family, studying and helping all I can. There is time to learn all.

The "Living Dead Man's" book speaks of a "Churchly Conventional Heaven." Maybe it does exist, but we haven't seen it, and we have consoled many who were hunting it. I, however, have never travelled far, but will travel later. Growth is what we seek now. The "Living Dead Man" was old and wise before he came over here, so he had a right to travel more than we. His book has made a deep impression on us here. Grandma E. was especially interested. She and Harry are most congenial. Perhaps she would like to write now, so I will be the link that guides your hand from now on, and let each of those who wish so much to talk to you do so.

HELEN

NOTES TO MAMIE[25]
FROM GRANDMA E.

35

 am your old grandma, Mamie, but Helen had better hold the pencil.[26] It does not seem long since you took me home on the train and were so thoughtful and kind to me. I neither look nor feel old now, but I am no less your grandmother, for all that.

Ask your mother to look for that portrait of me she has stored away somewhere, and take it to Nellie. Nellie loves me very deeply. She remembers me in a way that is very gratifying. Lucia should be generous as well as charitable with Nellie, as they both belong to our workers here, and should feel their comradeship while there.

Let Lucia gather up a few keep-sakes and take them with her to Nellie. What other richer gifts she has in mind she may send later, but I hope she will not meet Nellie now empty-handed. I know that a beautiful gift with sentiment behind it warms the heart. It will help me to grow here if my children are in sympathy and harmony.

Lucia has a generous heart, and her father's quick, impulsive nature; traits I have learned to appreciate

---

25 *This was Grandma Eames' nickname for Mary.*

26 *The first line of this letter was written in a finer hand than the usual style of these communications. - L.E.B.*

since coming here.

Your father, Lucia, takes a keen interest in all you strive to do. Of all our children you are nearest his heart, because he understands you best.

Give Gardner[27] the portrait of his father. He longs for it, and it can do him no harm. Lucia need not fear making mistakes about dividing her keepsakes wisely. With you to advise, through whom we so easily pass our own desires, she can't go far wrong.

Ask your mother to try to give Nellie the little dressing table she used to have. This will be hard to do, I know, but it is the thing Nellie wishes most, and the gift will warm her heart as no amount of money would. Besides, the sacrifice on Lucia's part will lift her higher here than any other one thing I can see. I hope she is now strong enough to make this gift.

We watch so eagerly every step she takes toward unselfishness, her father and I, and are made as happy as we were when as a baby she learned to walk between us. Each wavering step toward the right path is rejoiced over and applauded with an interest and enthusiasm no young parents could exceed.

She must not forget that she is our first child to set her feet on the upward path. We should have felt ourselves failures but for her. You see it is pathetic, don't you, that we feel this sense of failure about our children? Judson is not a failure, but we did not train him. Charles is a good boy, but we have left none who have repaired our mistakes, so we look to Lucia to do more than her share. If she only does that for us we may rest easy, and feel happier about the work we failed to do.

Thank you for writing all this. I see you will not fail with your boy, Mamie. He is quite a remarkable child already, and with our continued help should accomplish many fine things.

---

[27] *One of Mary's uncles.*

Perhaps I may come again some day. I appreciate the loyal devotion to my memory, and I shall strive to merit all you have given.

L.C.E.

CITIZENS
OF THE WORLD.

36

November 16, 1914

ll right, Sister, it's Helen. You see how much more easily we come to you after the duties have been done. Harry wishes to talk more. . .

It's about the less personal work, Sister. Each individual has two branches of work, both equally important to himself as a progressive soul. One pertains to his smaller individual development. The other is what is required of him as a citizen. We classify in this manner, as it makes our meaning clearer to you. Now, when we are willing to become citizens of the world we live upon, certain sacrifices are demanded as a guarantee of faith. We must serve our fellows as a community as well as individually.

Each unit has two sorts of duty, the larger being the secondary in case of personal emergency only. One may never lose sight of his civic or impersonal duty, because his future life can be assured through that alone, whereas the smaller duty is not sufficient to insure him against individual extinction, as it may be purely selfish. A public service cannot so be if it is sincerely performed. One presupposes sincerity in either case.

Now when any of you has mind enough to grasp a problem of national ethics or civic reform, by that fact alone you are made a member of the class of public servants, and mingled with your intimate family duties and pursuits there must run a strain of active interest in a larger life. It must be your neighbor's welfare you study, along with your own; your city's interest and progressive life; your nation's attitude toward all human interests both at home and abroad. This will keep your brain and heart open to the larger service required of all who have capacity. A man's or woman's duty is defined by that same test; capacity to do and be better than some other, less richly endowed. The plan of the entire universe seems to entail working each individual up to his capacity, without either strain or slack; just an even, steady pull, each according to his ability; no more, no less.

As soon as one's soul is illumined by a glimpse of truth it must assume the obligation of such illumination, must *live* it. No one is responsible until he has comprehension. Only then does the "Law" begin to act. An unseen duty does not exist, but once perceived it becomes imperative. That is why it is both stupid and unkind to judge another by our own standards. I am my own best judge, my only best judge. Can a child judge a parent? Can a criminal understand an Emerson? All great teachers have spoken of this, but their words were empty sounds to all but those who were enlightened. Slowly, very slowly the race evolves, circling round and round, ever higher. All are needed to help the mass to keep the pace.

You will see, as you lighten your barque of personal freight, how much each may do toward the general welfare. Keep on passing out your extra goods and chattels to those who still need toys to keep them happy. Children need content and undisturbed play-time. That, too, is a part of growth. Who can say but that the greatest seed of all lies germinating deep within, while the child-heart sits in the sunshine playing with its toys? So, don't be scornful of those to whom their toys seem good. They are growing. Later their adult duty will claim them for its own, as yours does now. The only fault in toys arises when they are cherished after their owner has grown beyond them. No one of you can tell the exact moment when the dormant, unseen seed will push its way up into the air and sunshine, a living, green thing. The greatest miracle of all is performed in the dark, unseen.

Plant life is a good illustration for soul life. We see only after the miracle has been performed. Its processes are secret and unseen always. Plant your seed then, and wait, with faith and hope. What you must do will come straight before you if you have eyes to see. Home missions always come first. In one's own house lie the materials to build one's character, to perfect one's soul. Are your eyes yet open, or are you still playing happily with toys? I need say no more to-night.

HARRY

STAGES OF DEVELOPMENT . . . CORRECTING EARLIER JUDGMENTS.

37

November 19, 1914

elen is here now. Let's try writing finer. . . . It's only one of the usual pauses to adjust the vibratory connections. All right now, Sister.

What Harry said last was not quite finished. He wishes me to tell of the things we have learned about the Law. First, you must know that we here live in groups or companies, working or studying along much the same lines; people between certain character or brain limits forming one group, those above or below belonging to other classes among those of their own sort.

When one belongs to an active group or class, one has neither opportunity nor leisure to drift beyond or outside, since strictly adhering to the point in hand is one of the main essentials of progress. Without concentrated attention one could not expect to master a study of anything, or accomplish any actual work. This fact alone will account for much apparent ignorance along other lines of work or study. We attempt only that which is at the moment within our intellectual grasp. We advance a step at a time. We strive to take each step firmly, and with absolute mastery.

We arrive on this plane of life at many different stages of development, from the sleeping infant to the sage. Between these extremes lies a vast area, peopled by students in every known stage of development. Those who pass the death gate may go directly beyond our reach, so that unless they happened to be personal friends in life, we never are aware that they are here. While no place here seems crowded, yet millions pass and repass. One might sit a lifetime, watching the procession. We pause sometimes, and glance at the long procession passing along our high road; but duty presses, and we may not tarry long in idleness here any more than you can there.

We who belong to the workers of the open field must relieve distress whenever we see it. Some day I shall also pass beyond this plane, when I shall have earned my holiday to rest with you and those I love. I sometimes long for that time, when I get a passing glimpse of what life higher up means for those fitted to live there. I am not discontented; I did not mean that. But sometimes even we grow weary from long continued work, and rest looks inviting. Harry says I work far too continuously, but I had far to travel, and wished to make sure I could have my rest and play-time on as high a plane as my own people could reach.

Many have gone higher. Even Harry lives always above my own working place. I live part of the time with him, but not half, or I would risk the loss of my connection with you. But let us lay aside personal things for the moment.

Harry wishes me to say that whenever you forgive those whom you fancy have injured you, you are placing under each a stepping stone to a higher life. It is never the injured party who needs pity, but the one who did the injury. It is in his soul that the weakness lies. Help those who have injured, or rather have tried to injure you. They are groping in the dark. Lend a hand. Do them all the service you can. The mean, the selfish, the miserly; these are the starving ones. Their souls are poor and crippled.

It is almost a subject for a smile to see how your sympathy goes out toward those troubled by physical hunger. The suffering of these even disturbs your sleep; while those whose souls are starving, shrinking, and shrivelling from lack of heart and generosity, you pass with an uncharitable glance only, and oh, how much more their need! A starving body bravely borne has no real loss to meet. But when a soul starves it faces the only real death in all the universe. Look deeper. Judge more wisely in your charities. A flannel shirt is a pleasant gift in winter to a freezing pauper, true; but a word, a look of sympathy, may save a soul from moral suicide. I wouldn't have you stop giving shirts, but only ask you to realize that the kind and patient word, the charitable judgment, is vastly more important. The poor we have always with us, even if our associates be exclusively millionaires.

See that your charity is always alert, and your eyes keen to see another's need.

Yes, Sister, I will answer questions now.

Harry has gone with the master on a tour, with a still greater teacher than Tee's brother. After they return perhaps we shall hear their experiences. Edith couldn't go, as John is in her charge; but Julia and Grandma E. went with them.

That book you read with Tee planted the seed of desire to look further into conditions here. Harry wished to find the records of his past lives, and Julia was going for study too.

I cannot say that I am lonely exactly, for I have you and Edith and my work; but I miss them. I had learned to depend on Harry for love and sympathy and conversations over questions of constantly occurring importance, so I miss him. I can't say when they will be back. I hope soon.

[Later.] Sister, don't be blue. It's all right. Cheer up! I love you, and I've just had a message from Harry. He says:

"Tell Sister we have all been together in other lives, in many combinations of relationship, so it is not strange we are so closely knit this time. And tell her John is one of those who will have a world message that he can speak in any of three ways this time, as he has earned that right. Tell her to teach him all she knows of art, as well as religion, that he may begin where he left off before. Oh, yes, John has been with you repeatedly, as I have, and Helen, and Tee too.

"I have been reading our four records, as well as Mamma's and Marie's, and have found out volumes of interest to us. Any or all of us may have lived one or two isolated lives, but we four belong to the same group. That is, our souls are about equally developed, and we gravitate toward each other repeatedly. . . .

"After one passes through every emotional combination sex and flesh are heir to, one can then know what others feel and are. One holds the keys which open human hearts, and we may then incarnate and live without any sex ties, having lived enough to lay aside any but friendly feeling. One's love expands only after having been satisfied completely in its sex and family relation. It can then overflow, and fertilize all who need sympathy and understanding."

Harry also has learned more about Catholic priests, and how fine their work is. The idea of a celibate life comes from a high ideal. It's what all souls aspire to; to live and serve without the selfish distraction of a family tie. The idea is splendid and true, but it's only a soul of vast experience who can live such a life perfectly. If any soul has not been previously satisfied, the strain is too great. It either takes too much will power to fight down the normal sex call, or else the man gives way and becomes what is called a sinner. He is not that; he is simply out of place at the moment. He took the teacher's task too soon; that's all.

When I spoke of Catholics before I was simply ignorant, and should never have given an opinion. I judged by my own small circle, and gave an untrue picture. I'm sorry, doubly so, as you read this narrow opinion to others. Please strike it from your book. I think Father Hughes as fine a soul as we have seen.

Sister, your loyalty after what we said makes us feel you are quite safe from any unworthy influence from here. As Harry says: "Sister never swallows us whole." Luckily, I add.

You can fancy how eager we are to learn all about Harry's reincarnation discoveries. This story will be most instructive and inspiring, as it enables us to get ourselves ready for further work. Now we can plan exactly the sort of work we need most to make us able to help others in our next earth life. It may be we shall separate widely in order to bring the same idea to many peoples by different avenues: through science, or teaching in the personal way a priest or preacher does. We shall plan our work here, then when we are quite prepared we shall descend and begin to live it out.

Sis, go to the lecture. Never shirk those things.

Au revoir,

HELEN

REINCARNATION . . .
THE PATH TOWARD
THE LIGHT.

38

November 22, 1914

elen is here. We wish to begin the story of Harry's travels, so I shall quote Harry direct. . . .

It is I, Harry.

I am in a real dilemma as to just where and how to begin; also what to tell and what to leave untold, especially the latter. Some ideas are so startling they overshoot the mark and lose their potency as stimulation to swifter, surer action. I find myself embarrassed by riches, which perchance you will fail to recognize as such. You may well imagine that the fact you pass these letters on deters us from giving much which we should not hesitate to hand over to you alone. I shall trust your judgment, as I must if I decide to give all I wish to.

I was able, with a teacher's help, to trace the course of my own soul backward several thousands of years; back, in fact, to that lost continent of Atlantis, where I left off, as it opened a vista too absorbing for present needs.

I saw no life in detail except those which were spent with any of you there now or those here with me now.

In company with Hughey I traced Tee's life path as far back as my own; also Sister's, Bess's,

Walter's[28], Mamma's and Papa's; seeing in addition where we first lived joint lives.

What I tried to find out was the general trend of each from its first vital or moral impulse reaching toward the light, as well as what made the fundamental desires of each which carried over from life to life. These differed in most of us, yet drew us back repeatedly to similar environment.

Mamma has been with Papa over and over again, because he supplemented her nature, and gave her congenial environment for work she felt a deep desire to perform. With the intense spirit of the fanatic she has given life after life for her ideal of human liberty. Liberty of mind and soul has been her slogan for a thousand years. Always a woman, she has frequently almost unsexed herself for her dream of liberty; personal, individual liberty even more than civil liberty. Hers has been the effort to be and do whatever she felt in her innermost soul was right and just. She, along with nearly every other member of the family, has suffered martyrdom in dozens of different ways.

That blood-sealed idea seems to lift a soul above selfishness sooner than any other. To give all one has to life and opportunity is doing one's utmost to further Truth as we vision it. It was this dream of freedom and personal liberty which made the Christian martyrs such a power. Mama has given her life repeatedly, but even giving up at times ceases to be the most effective means of progress. A soul grows vain of that as well as of other things. It gets to be a sort of sanctified habit, and must be eliminated.

Mamma's present faults spring from an inner conviction of being right at bottom every time. A certain balance must be maintained, even in virtue. No soul can endure too much virtue consciously. One

---

[28] *Bess (a sister) and Walter (a brother) were both still living at the time the letters were written.*

is apt to make uncharitable judgments. One can see too many fools and weaklings about. In fact, the habit of martyrdom breeds intolerance.

Mamma is learning. Some day she will arrive at the point where a smoker will fail to rouse a spark of criticism, or even of interest. When that day comes she will have learned what she is living for this time. Understand me, it's not the smoke that is bad or good, but what she feels about it, which concerns her. Her attitude is simply a relic of that fanaticism which repeated martyrdom breeds.

She has the vision of what she died for; personal liberty, not for herself alone, but for each and all.

Think it over.

HARRY

MORE ON
REINCARNATION . . . **39**
MAKE USE OF WHAT YOU HAVE.

November 27, 1914

elen is here. Harry is ready with more information about his travels and study.

It's now Harry. As I said before, I spent much of my time and study on the records of our family, collective as well as individual life history. As the "Living Dead Man" explained in his letters, the past is preserved in records as indestructible as existing life itself, and one's past is easily read if the will power is strong enough to magnify the pictures which lie, layer upon layer, on the tenuous material used to preserve them.

One may see any section of one's previous existences at will, like a sort of moving picture, plus the revival in one's heart of each emotion which accompanied the circumstance. This is an improvement on the earth's picture shows, which rarely stir my emotion beyond that of interest or amusement, and frequently not even that. Having sketched the manner of becoming conscious of one's own past, I shall now go on with the account.

I was able to follow not only my own past, but that of each member of my family as well as my wife. It was not only a most fascinating and absorbing task, but tremendously inspiring to be able to trace from primitive impulse the development of one's conscious, awakening soul; to note the sort of

127

thing which let in light from time to time; to observe which experiences taught truth, and which only befuddled the mind and reason. This was worth more than anything else I can mention as a comparison.

Once it was the devotion of a dog which taught me what real love might mean; a love without hope of reward, just devotion pure and simple. Another time it was a long prison sentence which taught me what freedom - real freedom - was. That showed me that no one is a prisoner except he shut his own heart away from love and pity and the desire to help.

You have before you a wonderful example of this same idea in Helen Keller, who is a living witness of the freedom of a soul. Imprisoned apparently beyond hope, behind the closed door of sense, eyes and ears gone, one would say all was lost in despair. There is no prison flesh can build which has power to enclose and stifle a soul who knows the Law. Unselfishness is the key unlocking every closed door. Unselfishness is only another name for love.

Why are any unhappy? Simply because they are thinking of themselves first. There is neither destruction nor pain nor failure of any sort that the soul who loves has not the power to dispel. Study that statement, please.

In all my study this one thing stands out as if written in lines of fire:

We are our own, and what is more our only destruction.

God lies within every one of us, waiting till we discover His presence; then, like the small child who discovers his father in hiding, with a glad cry we clasp our own. We too are God, which means that within every heart that beats there lies the power to do and be all that any man on earth has ever been or done. "What man has done man may do."

It is as though we sat in the dark with an electric switch within arm's reach, which when touched would send a flood of light about us. The energetic, curious person, sitting so, would feel about, expecting to find the means of light, while the inert would sit quietly accepting the dark as inevitable, or lamenting loudly about his desolate condition. Expect the best, then hunt for it with vigor.

Another thing I discovered was how frequently I had made similar mistakes along parallel lines; in short, how slow I was to grasp an idea. I seemed to sink before the same situation over and over again, because I had not the brain to grasp underlying principles.

To illustrate: Two and two sticks of wood equalled four sticks of wood, but two and two apples baffled all my mental equipment. And when it came to two and two acts I sat down in despair and gave it up. This is an illustration merely.

The fundamental principles underlying any law follow life in every form, and what human beings take so long to learn is the fact that the Law exists and acts always the same, through an endless variety of conditions.

The Law is simple, but its aspects are manifold, each aspect appearing to us like another law. We look always at the surface of things. Even people of intellectual development do so. One has to dig but a little way beneath the surface to discover the common root.

I have often watched a fly which had entered a trap by an opening plenty large enough to afford its exit also. Did the fly sit down quietly and figure out how it got in there, and then reason that if it got in it was equally able to get out? Not at all. It flew distractedly about, panic stricken, luring curious companions into its self-sought prison.

One may smile at the folly of the fly, but how much farther has the human evolved beyond the fly's reasoning power? Behold the European War! Did any of the rulers of Europe sit down quietly and reason out the situation? Not one! Yet any one of them had intelligence enough to see that a war never yet advanced any nation, either victor or vanquished, any more than any other form of destruction has advanced them except that what remains is too weak to destroy anything at the moment, and so directs all its energy toward constructive employments.

When hatred has destroyed all it can, the idea of brotherhood flourishes for a time, simply as the normal reaction. The world of men hasn't learned that brotherhood pays, and that hatred and conflict do not. It's a simple law, but they do not see it yet except in isolated groups of individuals.

They only half believe that honesty pays. But some people do enough to allow commerce to flourish. I sometimes wonder at the colossal stupidity of the human race as a whole. Evolution is painfully slow.

But to return to the topic we started. In records of the past I noted a certain similarity of motive, and a strong desire among us to develop, which accounted for our simultaneously gravitating toward rebirth so often. We are earnest in our desire to know the "truth." Conventions have not deterred us from thinking things out for ourselves. Individual independence seems strongly marked. Like the Yankee, "we want to know."

Fear does not exist on the mental plane. I wonder why the superstition of fear exists with us at all. It is always an indication of ignorance. You do not fear death now, nor hell, both being transitory states; merely incidents along the path. Why then fear poverty, or sickness, or loss of sight, or property?

One must play the game. The child who hugs his ball within his pocket's shelter, fearing he may lose it if he plays the game, we know is silly. Worse! He robs himself of not only the health exercise brings, but the joy of the game, the exhilaration of contest. He is stupid in the extreme who is unwilling to risk his possession by throwing it into the open, letting someone else share the game his treasure has power to launch.

Let us be simple and enjoy playing life's game, regardless of the possible loss of our ball. The real treasure, of course, is what our souls can extract from the play.

Each must use whatever he is, or has, in as many ways, and for the benefit of as many people, as possible. I don't mean to say one should crowd one's talents or attentions on outsiders, but that the personal gifts or possessions we enjoy must be cultivated, and divided or shared with those whose lives touch ours, and whose need seems to require what we can give.

Hoarding is criminal as well as stupid. It is a sort of colossal selfishness no one can afford to indulge in. Haven't you intelligence enough to realize the truth of that statement?

When you have two chairs, and are able to occupy but one, and there are others with no chair, a very little arithmetic will show that the extra chair in your possession is out of place. To be still more explicit: this house has at least three or four beds too many. Three or four guest beds should be enough in any house. Exceed that number and you are doing someone else, somewhere, a wrong. Those extra beds must be used. Look about you and see who needs them. It is the same with fifty other things. Get them moving. Pass them on. Don't be stupid, please. Give away more clothes, rags, junk of all sorts. Let most of your keepsakes be in the hearts of other people.

I repeat, don't hoard anything from furniture to ideas. The real things are free. Love, service, ideas, landscapes, God; all are or should be common to all.

I talk too long.

HARRY

THERE IS NO INJUSTICE . . .
AND NO TORMENT EQUAL
TO A BAFFLED DESIRE TO SERVE.

40

December 3, 1914

ister: I will repeat what I told you before, and you destroyed as merely personal. It applies to anyone else who has lost all or part or any of their five senses. The Law never varies.

I told you that it puzzled us to know why, before you had time to commit any sin, scarlet fever had destroyed your eyes to such an extent you had to forego all those pursuits that you were both fitted for and loved best. We had been here long enough to see that the loss of sight always indicated brutal selfishness and injury of another. Why then were you stricken, when you were guilty of neither of these?

Harry always insisted that reincarnation would solve many baffling problems, did we only accept that theory of life. We knew there was no injustice in the universe, hence there must be somewhere a perfectly good and just reason for your loss of sight; a moral reason. There are no physical expressions anywhere without a moral of spiritual cause. So without any prejudice we started to discover the Law. Harry found a teacher whose task is to read the records of life, past and present, and by these records he found that the individual soul lived many earth lives in order to gather its education, or evolve its God-self.

He saw away back in the experience of your soul

that you had wantonly put out the eyes of a little child, then abandoned it to its fate. For this brutal and selfish act, you, because of your ignorance, must learn that such an act was wrong. Being ignorant and blind of soul, it took a long, long time to teach you the real lesson of blindness. Four times you were born blind, and always you were unhappy and mourned your cruel fate. Three times then you were given partial sight. Still, through life after life, you thought only of your own privations, your own lack of opportunity to be great. Then little by little the bitterness, melted out of your heart. Resentment at your condition passed into a cheerful acceptance of conditions. Only within a few years now, has light dawned in your soul.

Now you feel a sort of despair that the greatest loss of all comes through your being helpless to serve those you love. You cannot read to your boy, nor to your husband, nor to your parents, whose sight is going also. This hurts. This impotence when help is needed is maddening, and this suffering has paid your debt. You will never be blind again.

Not what you lost, but what you could not give! Not what any of us suffer, no matter where, for our personal privation, but what we are powerless to give others, is the illumination of the Law.

So long as those without money bemoan their personal privation they will be poor over and over again. Until they see that poverty prevents them from helping those in a worse plight they have missed their lesson.

To serve our fellows is one of the two fundamental means of growth. Until we accept that, we remain in the kindergarten of life, and suffer blindly. There is no torment equal to a baffled desire to serve. After we learn that, we can enter the class which has dominion over all the elements of earth. We then may yield real power.

Jesus taught this law of service over and over, to a blind people. They, like you, worshipped gain. Success meant the possession of material things. The conception of success with most of you has not altered much. You know nothing of power - real power. You can torture a dog or a man until through fear of physical violence he obeys your command. Power could have obedience more complete through the voluntary service of both dog and man because of love. True love casteth out fear, and there has now and then been a man so fearless, so full of love for all living things, that he masters them, and to him comes no harm from any. There is a brotherhood of life which will give one dominion over the earth.

What is power? Surely not the ability to trap and cage a wild beast. That is only stupid force. Power is that quality in the soul of man which can make a wild beast lie beside one and lick his feet as a dumb symbol of devotion, and a great love is the only means of achieving such power. When a king is so strong that his subjects will lay aside selfish desires for his sake, he is truly a king.

Love and absolute brotherhood between man and beast is the solution to all the earth's problems. Cheerful, loving service is far ahead of the sullen task compelled by a lash of any sort.

How blind and stupid most people are. It is pitiful. Forgive your enemy. It is the only way to help him learn his lesson. Serve him. Be patient. Forgive seventy times seven.

How many of us forgive at all? Someone has hurt us, we who are kind and good and well meaning. Therefore that one is mean, cruel, base. We hate and shun him. We leave him alone and thank God that we are different. Are we?

Even a very low type of man finds it exceedingly difficult to injure a person repeatedly who bears no resentment and even performs services for him. The voice of the God within cries out to his other self in the heart of one who returns good for evil, and in time the injurer must bow to its power.

Love, not hate, conquers.

The God within the heart of man is the only ruler who is victorious beyond any doubt. The tangled skein of human life will all come straight when each has learned that one truth. How long will it be before more than a pitiful handful at a time will learn that?

HELEN

December 10, 1914

Yes, Sister, we are both ready to write, Harry first.

Tell Marie[29] I am delighted with her life as she has been living it. She may be certain I know and feel all her trials, as well as see and applaud her successes. We live nearer now than before, which seem strange, doesn't it? But clearer understanding always brings people closer together. She may do whatever seems best in her judgment, and bank on my being pleased and satisfied every time. She can't possibly fail because she has the true spirit of unselfishness. I marvel at the beauty of her soul every day she lives.

Tell Marie I am learning from her, and trying to make good here as she does there. She is one of my most powerful inspirations. A wife like her is a gold mine to any man if he only knew it. Tee knows, and I know, but few can see it. It takes men ages to see what they owe to the woman soul. But they are waking up all along the line, up here as well as with you.

Tell Marie that A.[30] won't hurt her in any way so long as she can keep her own spirit happy and serene. A's darker nature is powerless against any who stand in the sun. Marie knows what that means.

---

[29] *Harry's wife who remarried after his death.*

[30] *A. was apparently a family acquaintance. He was not a relative. Surviving family members do not recall his identity.*

Just let her live her life as usual, and she will be impervious to harm from anyone.

Do try, Sister, to rise above that angry feeling A. inspires. It is stupid, for it hurts your own soul. A. can harm none but himself unless the others allow hate and unkind judgments to enter into their own hearts. Only what is within can hurt us. No danger, no harm comes from without. Everything, good or bad, comes first from within our own natures. This attracts to itself either good or bad. Like seeks like. This is the Law. If you would love and pity A. instead of knocking and hating him, you would call out all the natural good in him, and so help to save his soul. Can't you at least try this method? You all know the Law. Why don't you live it? Never say a word again in criticism. Keep still and pray for more love. See how much it will improve the situation. It is the only way out. Do, we beg of you, try. "Buck up!"

HARRY

LISTEN TO YOUR INNER VOICE.

41

December 15, 1914

elen is here now, and Harry will be here later. He has asked me to write first this time, as he has important work on hand.

When you were so busy at home yesterday, we were making up our next year's outline, looking ahead to see in what direction it would be best for you to travel. The future stretches out ahead of you in a sort of picture. Yet, unlike the past, it is capable of slight alterations by us, and could be entirely changed by you were you to set your will power against it.

You see, life is like a game of chess. With some types you can know in advance just what sort of moves they will make under given conditions, and what conditions they will create under certain combinations of emotions or feeling. We can, for instance, tell in advance with absolute certainty what some people will do if confronted with poverty or loss of any sort. A fine, strong nature, with a closely knit will, never fails to rise and put forth greater effort than before; while a weak, selfish nature whines and then looks for an easy berth, a pleasant way out. To these latter, physical ease and freedom from responsibility are always sought, and excuses given for accepting them when even personal honor is sacrificed.

No strong soul ever yields to dishonor, no matter

what the pressure from without. Only a weakling prefers physical ease to death when such an issue presents itself.

Will is free, always. But only the strong make destiny or the path carved out of life by will . . . will and desire.

There is no future we can read in advance for a strong soul, because at any moment he may alter the course of his life and create a different environment. We cannot see the inner flash of conviction which directs one soul this way, and another that.

When anyone becomes aware of the fact that he is in a school, with tasks before him which must be mastered, he then gravitates toward the environment where this or that lesson can be best learned. There is a center in each, which if perceived, will be a sure guide to one's best development. Like a magnet it will draw to one all the requisite tools or conditions for the performance of one's necessary work. It is in very truth the voice of God, and it comes only from within. We must listen to that inner voice. It is there, if we only knew, or had faith to believe.

Look at the history of all so-called "Holy ones." Contemplation, silence, prayer, retirement, were large factors in the life of each. Why? They were waiting in the silence for the voice of God to speak from their own center.

We prattle a lot of God, but how many realize for a moment that it is the personal presence of God at the center of each which enables him to exist?

God is Life. God is the Creator, and he creates constantly, continuously, throughout the universe. That is the secret of life. God is behind and through everything, from a rock to a man, planet, or sun. All have life. All vibrate. All move. Law is the will of God. It is the fundamental impulse of living, the push from within.

Force is the greater unit of life. Or, putting it another way, a forceful man is one who has gathered gradually to his center more of God, more of creative power. As any soul opens his mind to truth, more light flows into him, through him. God is within each; but not all of God, only a fragment. The plan is to add to this fragment from without until it becomes greater and greater. By looking within we become aware of the nature of God or Life. Then we may recognize him when we see him without.

When one "knows God" he has the key to all wisdom, for thereafter he gathers only true knowledge, and encumbers his soul with nothing valueless.

Knowledge is power. Why? Because one is then carrying no weights whatever, but is free to advance and to serve. One is like a splendid athlete stripped for battle or contest; every ounce counts. There is no waste anywhere, no drag or impediment. One can then carve his own fortune, direct his own destiny. He is then Free.

When one has this power, one can master circumstances as easily as a man wades a brook. Jesus had the power to conquer an earthly kingdom, but with that power came the wisdom to see how paltry and childish such ambitions are. The possession of dead riches is unworthy the desire of an adult human soul. The living treasure of the hearts of men was the kingdom Jesus sought; the kingdom of Heaven within each human heart.

Locked within each living thing lies the treasure, God. Jesus tried to open these inner doors and disclose to each soul its eternal riches. Love only can penetrate into the inner recesses of any soul; love, patient and hopeful. The doors may be thick, but no matter how far below the surface of a man the light is buried, it is surely there, waiting discovery, liberation. If it were not there, life, even of body, would be extinct. "While there is life there is hope," is only too true; hope that today someone may love enough to open that heart and free the imprisoned glory.

When we criticize or condemn, we are thickening the wall between that person's God and the light

139

without. When we insist upon his goodness, his better nature, we are removing some of the entombing material, and helping him toward freedom and light. We must believe in every one's best. That is one of the greatest lessons Jesus tried to teach; charity toward all. "Father, forgive them, for they know not what they do." He knew those who persecuted him were building walls about their own hearts, darkening their own lives.

It is almost Christmas time. Let us all think of what that means, and live the Christ life more fully. Let us try during this year ahead of us to love with a deeper, truer, more intelligent love, serving all who touch our lives, by a splendid faith in their best. Let us have the humble spirit of one who knows his own limitations. No one can feel superior so long as there lies in his own mind an uncharitable thought for any other.

Give yourselves this test of faith, and see how you can emerge from it. We are all children of God. Some of us are older and wiser than others, but we belong to the same family.

Let us join hands and wish each other God-speed.

HELEN

When you gather round the table Christmas Day, remember us here, and feel that we too share in your Christmas cheer. We love to feel you count us in when you are all together.

We feel happier this year than ever before, and hope you realize what these letters mean to us.

With all the love and service we have the power to give, we wish you a Merry Christmas, and a happy, useful and prosperous New Year.

HELEN and HARRY

All of us join in this greeting.

140

THE POWER OF ART . . .
BEAUTY IS
NEVER USELESS.

42

January 17, 1915

elen is here. Oh, yes, I've been wanting to get you for days. It's for the news about Harry. Some thing quite wonderful has happened to him. He has gone with Hughey for a trip through space to study other planets, and will go right on with his music study, getting deeper into the heart of it by seeing its force or power in the eternal rhythm of planets and worlds, and all sorts of big whirling bodies.

Hughey and Harry are studying the relation of music to force, or that push from behind which implies motion, the evolving of things. You know motion or vibration is continuous, and each atom evolved and combines into forms, and as things progress they sing, or create tones, musical or otherwise, as the motion is smooth or jerky, rhythmic or broken. Nothing lives or moves without sound. Even vegetation sings its growth song. The ripping and snapping of an opening bud is a sort of music, were your ears keen enough to hear.

Seeing all this, we got the idea that behind all growth, which is another term for evolution, lay a great principle connected with music; in fact, that music was a part of life itself. Now what we wished to know was its effect on growth; whether it is only a result, and not co-equal or coordinate with cause.

These are not the right words. I will try again;

141

whether music is so united with life force as to be a part of it, and not a by-product merely; that it is really what you would call useful material instead of a luxury or thing of beauty merely.

Beauty, we feel, is never a useless or ornamental thing. It is of deep and vital use. Trace anything back to its source, and one will find it a vital factor in the evolution or development of God. I know this sounds rather wild, but if God includes all life, then God is in the process of growth. Believing ourselves a part of Divinity, we study to understand the plan of this everlasting opening up and growing from the "in" outward, this continuous circling through life forms.

Of course it is simple and easy to say God is all, God is Life, God is Soul, and let it go at that. But within each unit we call individual there is a restless, poignant desire to know, to find out the why, and how, and when. No matter on what plane a soul may be, it is never content for long. The inward desire pushes it on to learn the enclosed truth, the hidden answer to the human question, why?

We say this is vital, and that is unimportant. We say art, music, acting, sculpture are all the ornamental, unimportant work of men. Did you ever stop to think that in the heart of the flower lies the seed of the plant? It's not the roots nor the leaves, but the apparent ornament of bloom, which is most vital to a plant. In its beauty is hidden its future.

The soul of a people lies in its art. In the so-called flower of its civilization, and away back of this, lies some vital truth yet undiscovered; the mechanical force, if you will, of the so-called ornaments of life. What inherent power has music, for instance, that being the aspect of art we study. It is this the two men have gone to seek out if they can find it.

You must go now. Tell Papa it is better here because we create our own sunshine.

HELEN

142

EACH SOUL HAS A SPECIAL PERFUME.

43

January 22, 1915

ll right, Sister. Thanks for waiting. I was with Grandma E. She is working in her flowers for knowledge of cures for spiritual ailments. You know what wonders are contained in odors; what a close link there is between the sense of smell and the emotions. People with you study little into this side of science, which we find so useful, as well as fascinating.

Mental states can be altered and controlled through the introduction of a perfume or disagreeable odor. Grandma, loving flowers as she does, drifted quite naturally into this study; and being also a born teacher, she uses her gifts in combination with wonderful results.

Each soul has a special perfume which seems a sort of personal property, and which will affect it more than any other. As you have guessed, yours is the tube rose. That belongs to you on your present plane, though the rose odor La France also belongs to you. If I were you I would discard any other perfume and stick to roses. They mean something, and can help you on your way.

Tee needs you, Sister. . . .

It's rather hard to keep from advising you to do things. That is why I stopped then. It is better for you to work it out for yourselves. You will give the best advice, I feel sure.

Tee needs you even more than he is aware. It may be wise for him to take a long rest, and look at life from a different angle for a while. He must do what looks best to him, remembering that a detour sometimes brings the revelation of an even better path upward. Detours matter very little if the main direction be kept; and when taken with faith and a desire to do and be what is best, they never fail to reveal finer things.

HELEN

OTHER PLANETS . . .
NEW INSIGHTS FROM OUTER SPACE: **44**
THERE ARE MANY ROADS TO GLORY.

January 26, 1915

s we promised, we are here. Harry will write now, or rather dictate, as usual.

I scarcely know how or where to begin my story, Sister. Hughey, Edith and I, with a great teacher who acted as guide, were taken to several other planets inhabited by beings who were once just people like us. I can't describe what they seem to be. They are infinitely finer, clearer-eyed, and more beautiful than we, being a race made up wholly of what we speak of as ideal; in coloring, form, grace of movement, and melodiousness of voice, just each a perfect human creature. But . . . and here all likeness ceases . . . absolutely devoid of material ambition, lust of power or possession. A race of students, living for the good of the race; utterly unselfish; able to train and use elements as we use carpenters' tools, yet seeing before them as much to learn apparently, as we do.

Seeing these people and glimpsing their horizon lifted my spirit beyond the fear of ever being depressed. Life, this big splendid unfoldment, is so tremendously interesting and inspiring, that one has no time to sit down and snap at flies. Just as if you were there watching some magnificent pageant you would be utterly oblivious to a mosquito biting your ankle. That is the way the petty bickerings and

145

heartaches of your lives look after a glimpse of that other. Life further on is so beautiful, so splendid, so full of work and power to do, it takes one's breath just to see it, and realize that we are candidates for that larger life if we keep on doing our best; keep on weeding out of our lives the non-essentials; keep on striving toward the highest we can conceive.

Each turn of the wheel brings revelation, an opening out of the higher path. What seems vital at one point a little further on drops out of the picture altogether.

Growth, change, is vital. Anything which tends to harden our outlines is suicidal. We are petrifying when we hold on to anything, either material, mental, or moral, after we get a glimpse of better things. We must leave our minds open to revelation, to change, to expansion. I feel we may have done you a wrong when telling you to hold to this or that form of work. Holding on to anything indefinitely is a dangerous attitude of mind. One's mind as well as one's heart should be kept expectant, ready to see the next lesson God presents.

I am not half so sure now as I was a short time ago, that I know what is best. I have seen whole systems melt and break up and apparently dissolve, and out of the chaos I have seen rise something far more beautiful, more subtly true than the first, and yet containing the same elements, the same life, the same big desire.

Having seen, I hasten back to you, not to unsay what I have said before, but to add a further word of hope. Through all life, all work, runs a golden thread of eternal truth; through each task, be it a duty or an art, a mere livelihood, or a love. The things we do are just differently colored and variously shaped beads on the same string. The Creator cares as much for the bead of clay or glass as the jewel of gold, but each must be strung on the thread of honest desire and unselfish devotion.

My horizon has opened out. I see now that music and so-called art work is absolutely the same as any other result of honest human effort. What matters in any work is the spirit back of it, the love we mix with it. Now it is possible, as I say, to love every sort of work equally, and to turn from one to the other without altering one atom in the combination.

What is our pet work or preference? It results merely from our childish idea that good is limited. A child likes only one or two sorts of food at first. Gradually it learns that food is meant mainly to sustain life, and there are many sorts of food capable of that service. It is so with work. What any work is for is to develop the soul and help mould character. We begin by doing only what we find most attractive. Later, as we progress beyond the infant class, we see that any and all work is good, if it be needed, and that the need of the work, not the desire of the worker, is its *raison d'etre*.

Character grows in any climate, but only by the adult mind can this truth be perceived. Human beings continually seek congenial environment, the work they love; when all they need is a realization of the principles of human development, and the desire to evolve. It is imperative that each soul give his or her utmost, no matter what or how, the main thing being that we give to the utmost.

If one possesses some great gift one should naturally cultivate that and share it generously. But unless one has the gift, the call is only for one's best. Use one's mind in selection of work, but if circumstances seem to hem one in, then do cheerfully the next best thing, knowing for a certainty all roads lead to the same goal.

Why do artists starve in garrets when there is so great a need for field hands? Simply because they are stupid, and believe there is only one road to glory. Do what needs to be done, whether it is in your chosen line or not. It is just as good a means of building fine things into your character as the work you prefer, perhaps better.

Life and growth are free and within the reach of all. Fit your work to your environment, and keep on

147

improving your methods. You see what I mean? Get the underlying principle of anything and you can then soon master all its combinations.

That's all for now. I see you are tired, Sister. Thanks.

HARRY

LEARNING FROM PAST LIVES . . . RUBBING IN TRUTH UNTIL IT REACHES THE BONE.

45

January 30, 1915

ere we are, Sister. You have learned the best way to us now, doing duties first. This always leaves your mind and heart open to our influences. Harry wishes to talk again. This time it is for Tee only:

Tee, old pal, let's have another heart to heart talk, which isn't possible, as I expect to do another monologue. I want to tell what I saw in your past lives, in order that you may save both time and energy in eliminating the unprofitable elements you have acquired along the unknown path.

I suppose the Creator knows his own business best, but there have been moments when I felt I could suggest improvements. For instance, had I been running affairs I should have been a little more open about this reincarnation plan of elevating the individual. Why let a soul boggle along blindly for numberless lives when just a friendly tip would have illuminated the whole situation and enabled him to plan with far less waste?

I can't for the life of me reconcile myself to the waste I see repeatedly going on all through nature, from acorns and seeds to people. Of course I'm no such fool as to imagine I could have planned things better. But being limited in vision I see apparent waste all along the line. However, that is neither here nor there, such discussion being "jolly" pure and simple. God knows; I don't. That's the whole thing in a nutshell.

Well, to continue. A man's memory of his plural past would save repetition of mistakes, as it takes numberless incidents of the same type to cut a dent deep enough to mould conduct.

For instance, if you were aware that you had been born and bred a tyrant or ruler repeatedly, you would examine carefully into the qualities likely to develop as a consequence, and watch with keenest interest the mental and moral warpings which are the logical fruit of such environment. Intolerance and self-will being the commonest traits developing under these conditions, one should in each subsequent life make an effort to cultivate such opposite tendencies as would balance the character.

He who is master oftener than slave, develops the selfish pleasure of the monarch, and enjoys doing rather than being, giving rather than taking. I have my doubts about its being better to give than to receive. I find it requires a far higher type of man to accept favors with dignity and grace than it does to shower blessings on a flattering populace.

Of course there is a giving which is splendid, and a taking which is degrading, but many of us have not yet reached the stage where we enjoy accepting from others. We have this big thing yet to learn: to be ennobled by a favor, humbled by giving.

We must give that which we cherish most, ourselves, our ideas, our privacy, our sacred reserves, all with love. . .

You desire what your heart cries out for, and should Fate deny you, life would be more or less a makeshift. Isn't that true? Could you ever give up your chosen work gladly? Not yet, I fancy. I didn't. No man does until the truth has been rubbed in so often that it reaches the bones. But if you knew and believed, as I do now, that one does not need one's fancied heart's desire to get the utmost out of life, that any life spent chasing one's heart's desire is pure waste, one would sit down and figure out just what would net him the most progress in the long run, and forget everything else of a strictly personal nature.

Far be it from me to coerce any human being, but I will lay open your past in its main points and let you look at it.

You owe a great deal to John. He has been your stepping stone to success over and over throughout the past, and this is your first opportunity to repay him for these repeated favors. It looks to me as though you would have a great chance to make good. Sister is also in his debt, and it is up to her too.

Your instinct would suggest there was a duty in that quarter, and, being parents, you would see in convention and added help. But it strikes me that a knowledge of facts would help even more and preclude the chance of any mistake. John is the one person you two are put here to further on his way. Whatever move brings more into his life is the move you should make. You both will best further your ultimate progress by seeing to his.

This is the main subject about which I wished to speak. Think it over, Tee, and you, too, Sister. Be sure you do everything gladly, freely, and because you honestly wish it. Otherwise it is all wasted sacrifice with a sting in it. A shadow of regret renders worthless; remember that.

Better trot right along as you are unless you can hand over your entire output without a qualm or reservation of any sort. If you can hand over everything, then his debt is paid in full, and you two are again free.

How is it?

HARRY

151

BELIEVE IN CHANGE AND GROWTH . . . THE GOAL IS TO BECOME, NOT TO GET.

46

February 1, 1915

s we are so far along the road to self-knowledge, I wish to say something more about the difficulty of seeing and doing what is best in the ultimate.

Being aware that I am of necessity a most imperfect product, I have sometimes an almost panicky feeling of self distrust. But after sitting down quietly and taking my bearings, I see that while I am in a most humiliating state of partial development, I may, in spite of that fact, be nearer the light than you, and so I am in a position to help you at least a little way toward illumination.

You are blind. I am just opening my eyes a trifle. Then if I refuse to give what I have, however pitifully small the gift, I am vain, and therefore hold back that little because of its smallness, when perhaps you could only receive that much, and more would pass your comprehension.

I want you to know that I do not preach to you as from an eminence, for I am lifted only the merest trifle above your own range of vision, seeing merely a bit more of the vast horizon we all long to achieve. I beg you won't take the small fragments of truth I write as the gospel of final truth. I only pass you the best I have, with the assurance of a sincere desire to help, and the belief that one's progress is never ending, but is, in fact, continuous, toward

152

Godhood.

Always believe in change and growth, as well here with us as there with you. As we evolve we perceive the higher law, law being progressive as well as other things. I want to make this quite clear to both you and Tee.

Another thing I wish to ask of you is never to take any statement from me without first testing it out in the crucible of your own highest judgment. It is difficult to transmit ideas across the border of differing life elements, and errors often occur through no fault that can be avoided. Up to now these errors have been so few as to count but little. However, I realize the danger of possible mistakes and errors as our work widens out, and I want to warn you to allow for such possible accidents. Common sense is your one safeguard. Accept nothing which fails to pass that test, and you are safe.

Of course we are all happy that our small efforts have proved so helpful, and this makes us feel that we may do even better with your help. What people need is hope and comfort, and the conviction that life is continuous, both before and after death. The more people who believe this, the sooner will arrive the age of brotherhood. One's ambition must be transferred from material success to spiritual insight. Work to *get* must be altered into effort to *become*. Happiness follows the one who is on the upward path of *becoming*.

Of course one should be a doer, but one must also *be*. To do the decent thing one is just obliged to be decent. Be decent then first, or the veneer of doing decently will some day crack off and show the sham beneath, and to be discovered a sham is about the greatest humiliation one can undergo.

To the one who has fought the fight for self mastery sympathy is easy, so if you find yourself judging some fellow traveller harshly because of some particularly mean trait, that will be proof positive you yourself have never conquered it within your own heart. For if you had, you would realize

153

the struggle entailed, and so accord a sympathy both deep and sincere. The victor is always generous, and in moral conflicts the victory is gained by such a narrow margin invariably, that one feels he has escaped only by the grace of God, and so feels a true sympathy for the one who must fight the same bitter and perilous battle with his inner enemy. No one ever wins an easy victory. It takes his utmost effort, and the result rests upon a hair's breadth, so no one can feel superior to his neighbor.

Give each struggling soul the helping hand of a kindly sympathy. He needs all he can get, and then may fail. Do you care to be the one who helped his failure? Are you in a position to cast the first stone?

Each harsh thought we indulge in is a drag on the soul who is battling for his eternal life. How cowardly in anyone to cripple another, either before or during his conscientious struggle to master his inner enemy. How dare we, when we know we shall reap what we sow? How dare we throw that boomerang? No one who *knows* oppresses in any way the weak. I hate to appeal to your desire for self preservation, but I can.

You may save your life by willingly giving it up, but you lose it permanently by saving it, by sacrificing another. You gain by giving, not by grasping. The miser is the greatest pauper of them all. But I have spoken of this law often before.

Adios,

HARRY

A TRUE MUSICIAN
MUST HAVE
A WORTHY MESSAGE.

47

February 7, 1915

ll right, Sister. I'm here, Helen. To-morrow is my birthday, and we shall celebrate it by a visit with you all. Let us have music in the evening, and some violin things. I have been feeling as if I might some day play with John. He is the type to make a famous artist, and may carry our message to those you could not reach with words. Music penetrates deep into the fundamental elements of being, and so there may be a way to reach each living heart.

There always is some way, only we haven't realized that. Music being an integral part of life itself, it must have great stirring power. Train John's hands, and his visual technique of music. Before he is given a violin let him learn to read music, and have primary lessons in harmony. Lay a broad foundation.

You see in any branch of art one should first train the muscles before intentional technique begins. I will explain. Any occupation which trains the hands to do skillful work and accurate tasks will fit those same hands for other work. A painter can be trained by the use of carpenter's tools. The eye grows keen and the hand efficient. With the violin one's ear is quite as important as one's eye, and hence lessons in singing and piano make a splendid foundation for violin work, as well as some manual training work.

Any occupation which develops the muscles and trains the ear and eye helps one immensely to master an instrument.

I want little John to take lots of time in preparation before he is allowed to handle the instrument we so love. The master feels John has a future before him we all may share, but it is your duty to look to his bodily welfare and the wholesomeness of his mind and heart.

Tee has his share also in John's development. He must not be allowed to develop in a one-sided way. All that tends to strengthen his body and make his mind clear and rational will be of untold value. To give the great message, the giver must be balanced, sane. The message is Love, and one must be able to live the life, to make it strike deep into other lives. Not blind love, but clear, patient, and understanding love, is what humanity needs, and music has power to stir the depths of any soul, and plant hope there, and fair desire, and ambition to achieve.

Too much time is usually taken for mastering the mechanics of any art. More time should be taken for developing the soul and mind and heart, that the message may be something besides exalted mechanics, gymnastics. A great violinist need not be such a marvelous gymnast. He may play quite simple compositions, and yet put a power of personality behind and through them that will affect the daily life of each listener.

The music of the future will be less complex, but it will grip the soul and deliver its message.

Teach John first the beauty and value of life. Let him live his message before he lets it speak. Then he will wield the only true power on earth. The whole great secret of Jesus lay in the fact of his clear vision, his love, his honest life. He lived what he believed, and his life is still doing its work. It is again that power of personality.

Why can't musicians grip the hearts of people more than they do, with the marvelous aid that is theirs? Simply because they neither live the life, have the

156

vision, nor love humanity. Most of them are vain and shallow and selfish, and pass away without leaving any permanent mark on history. A true musician must play his own compositions, and he must have a worthy message. There always has to be one great personality to go before as a pathfinder.

We hope John may find the path for the new music. Guard his life at all points, that he may learn only fine things, and keep him clean for the higher service.

These things are for you and Tee to work out together. You shall each do your own personal work, but your main use will be that you two form the pedestal on which stands the one who shall point out the new way, who will teach the vital truths of life through music. But for you the work could not be done so soon, so you are of deep importance to the project.

We know you will perform your part faithfully.

HELEN
and the MASTER

157

MORE ON REINCARNATION . . .
ADVICE IS USELESS
UNTIL IT IS DESIRED.

48

February 8, 1915

ll right, Sister, here we are for a birthday message.

Whenever we can have uninterrupted time to write, we wish to go on with the reincarnation story. Tee's was not finished, Harry says, nor yours. And Bess has a wonderful past.

Today, if you don't mind, I should like to tell Bess's[31] story. She has been marked for public service for many lives and has the "public habit" in spite of her gentle ways and speech.

She has belonged to the reformer class as far back as Harry went. She has been fired with the love of justice and individual liberty, throwing her all into the balance repeatedly. The habit of public service has rather crowded out the smaller personal point of view. She has developed beyond its need. So, Sister, you needn't worry.

The personal, narrow, home circle is all right for the individual with the narrow vision, and for the majority. But in all communities there must always be those who serve the mass outside the family circle. These broader duties tend to create a sort of carelessness of detail, which is irritating but not vital.

---

[31] *Bess married a minister.*

Of you all Bess has grasped the biggest idea and is living it. It is for this she is so well guarded as to bodily health and accident. Eugene[32] owes more to us than he realizes, who guard his environment for her sake, as well as for the sake of his own fine service.

Sister, your part is less showy, but not a bit less needed. Each according to his or her personal gifts. The main idea being identical, what is the use of the label? All are so very important.

HELEN

The following is M.'s[33] past history and its important points, as seen on Harry's journey into the past.

First, she has always been a woman, never a man. Sex, so far as we have been able to see, remains the same always.

Always a woman, she has evolved her independent personality through fighting her oppressors at all points. She has felt the sacredness and justice of individual liberty ever since she followed the teacher Jesus in his life. Her eyes were opened to the real meaning of his symbolic lessons. She grasped, even at that time, what he vainly tried to impress on all: the right of each soul to itself to be and think as it seems right from the standpoint of its own conscience. She felt the inner stir of that call for justice and liberty, and for this she was martyred many times, never being conquered by a despot.

Several times a nun, she learned what a cell can teach. She also learned the value of being a complete woman. The natural heart hunger of her starved nature as a celibate had made motherhood seem intensely desirable. She has not yet been satisfied,

---

[32] *Bess's husband, the minister.*

[33] *Probably Marie, Harry's wife.*

and will mother many more before her heart is surfeited.

As a Roman matron she took a keen interest in government, and her judgment was solicited by statesmen and patriots.

As a Puritan she was full of courage and resource, and led her frailer sisters in matters of common welfare, and also of steadfast faith.

Her latest life was led in New England in the eighteenth century. It was a long one, and she passed out in 1800.

Her faults were always those which are born of an intense personality and efficiency. Frugality degenerates into hoarding if not guarded against; capacity into a small form of tyranny, a tendency to boss others. These are now the only faults she need work upon. She has seen it, and is doing nobly.

She must realize, and does, I think, that each soul must be left to work out its own future. Love is about the only thing one is allowed to give without limit. Advice should never be offered until asked, as it is useless until desired.

Possessions of all sorts must be limited to the individual's ability to use them actively. One should not just sit in the midst of things, but live in a place where what is about one is in active service. No ornaments, either pictures or furniture, should be stored away. What cannot be enjoyed daily should be passed on.

The same is true about jewelry and clothes: pass them on. Keep things circulating and they don't die. This is a great truth. Things live and have a character as well as people. They absorb the personality of their owners, and give off the atmosphere or feeling of them. That is why one can feel at once whether the people who live in a place are fine and hospitable, or selfish and cold. Their things talk.

HELEN

WORK AND PLAY,
GIVE AND TAKE,
STRUGGLE AND REST.

49

February 19, 1915

ll right, Sister, this is Helen. Oh, I don't mind the criticism about being too wordy. It's true, and so I need it. If you would rather have Harry, he will come. Yes, I understand. I am not easily hurt when I feel you all love me. Feeling hurt is always the result of self-pity, and we don't indulge in that here.

Tee wishes to know about the souls of animals here. Perhaps I can answer before he arrives. We did not see any animals when I first came, but later they seemed to gravitate here, or perhaps we drifted elsewhere. It is hard to tell sometimes whether we ourselves move on, or the environment comes where we are. We all have power to create environment, and it may be that animals came when we felt a desire for them. Here one must have a hospitable spirit or there are no guests.

Oh, yes, any can be alone who so elects. Solitude is a simple proposition. We can create it anywhere. Anyone may, in any place, even with you. It only requires concentration. Just draw into your own shell. Each soul must be able to withdraw from others at times. No one can bear to give out constantly. He must take in once in a while; live rhythmically, in fact. Work and play, give and take, struggle and rest. Otherwise there is no balance, no poise. That is what ails you right now. You need to

161

relax and rest, to take in. Stop going for a while. Rest until the desire is strong to work again, no matter how long.

Don't fret about the dog, or the letters. Life is too fine and beautiful for that. Just sit happily and make plans for next summer. Harry says the western trip is perfectly feasible in spite of tales to the contrary.

Let other things slide for a time, and look up routes. Go somewhere every day alone with John, and begin improvements on the car. Don't do anything from a sense of duty for a while. It is not your duty to care for anyone but John and Tee. Enjoy the little boy while he is little. They are so soon grown up. This is your chance to be rested and jolly. Cut out everything which interferes with personal poise. You help none when nervous. I will write for you to-morrow, Sister. Yes, go now, and cheer up.

HELEN

OUR THOUGHTS
CREATE OUR
FUTURE ENVIRONMENTS.

50

February 20, 1915

arry is here to write Tee a personal letter.
. . .

Sister has been going down hill badly from overdoing, and Helen told her yesterday to quit. I want to add a word along the same line.

It's a true test of whether you are obeying the law when you find yourself either sick or nervous or blue. You know by any of these symptoms that you have drawn too heavily on your reserve vitality and let other people drain you. The remedy is perfectly simple. After work hours just disappear from people. Go into your shell and wait until you have time to fill up again. Relax your whole nature. Don't give anything out, either by sympathy or brain power, but lie quietly and make happy plans for the future.

Always remember the cheerful thought is what renews one's poise. Never brood over disaster. Forget it as rapidly as possible, and begin to make prosperous pictures of your future. Always picture the future, whether tomorrow, next year, or after death, as happy, as full of pleasant possibilities and happy incidents. We thus insure our future against evil happenings.

The plan of your happy future is a real concrete substance which must be destroyed on this plane before any contrary fact can be born on your plane.

Someone then must deliberately design your downfall or unhappiness, and work hard over here to that end before your own pictured future can be eliminated. Do you get me?

I will repeat to make sure. A personal plan or vision of a desired future is a visible, concrete thing here, holding solidly together so long as the creator of it holds it firmly in his brain. More than this the vision has power to build on your plane its counterpart in what you call fact, by a process of magnetic attraction. The law is one of the basic ones, and never fails unless the person is vacillating or weak.

Picture a certain form of disaster and you create it just as certainly as a stone falls through air when dropped from a height. The law is that we create by our own thought our future environment. The swiftness of the actual materialization depends upon the concentration of our thought, and the distinct quality of our vision, as well also whether we build it while feeling happy. Happy, cheerful states are splendid creators.

Sister makes the most solidly built plans, strengthened by frequent reviews and much detail. If she could plan as well for her restored sight she would get it.

Now, Tee, I will answer your query about the dog, Pat. Animals here are a most interesting study. They appear only when people seem to expect them. Pat came to me one day as I sat alone, thinking over my life with Marie. As I brought back the picture of Cuba I recalled Pat, and that moment I felt his tongue on my hand. He seemed overjoyed to see me, and has rarely left me since. I believe he has a soul, and I am trying to find out if he is a descending human, or a man in the making. I can't say. We are studying this in a class I belong to, and we gather data from all sorts of places. I sometimes feel he is a descending man, instead of a rising brute, because he does not obey. The lower orders obey instinctively, but man is a natural anarchist.

HARRY

GERMANY IN 1915:
WORLDLY SUCCESS
BUILT ON SAND.

51

August 10, 1915

ith confidence comes fair weather, and mind governs the planet in all its details; mind, which includes feeling as well. "As a man thinketh, so is he." As the world feeleth, so is it. The light of faith, held by a few souls, has more than once illumined the path of escapes when world disaster threatened.

Leaven is a sort of magic. Faith is like that. The great faith of a few has been able to lift a race, a race otherwise lost. Belgium today is more alive, more successful, than Germany, because her faith is backed up by the undying power of justice. Germany's faith makes for worldly success, but it is built on sand and cannot stand the flood which will come. Right and justice only are immortal. Any success not founded on them has no stability. You have but to look at history. Where material interests outweighed moral interests, that state was doomed. Only through moral integrity, the ideals of individual liberty, and a deep consideration for one's fellow men, can be secured the immortality of individual or nation. When the cry is to help instead of to dominate, both here and in all other lands, that day the earth sets its foot on the threshold of immortality, and man will rise to be broken on the wheel no more. One must lose one's life, or rather give one's life, to keep it eternally. That is, one must unselfishly give all one has for the general good; not for glory, but for right. To serve one's fellows is to build one's immortality.

Good luck and good cheer from all of us.

HELEN

KARMA.

52

September 13, 1915

ll right, Sister, we will talk now about the book. We selected C.L. for Mamma's helper, as we knew of no one else fit for such a task. She really cares, and whenever one can put heart into a work such work succeeds as no other can.

Let C.L. feel she has a future. We are all helping to train her for it, U.C. most of all, naturally, aided most efficiently by G.E. The latter is C.L.'s guardian spirit, and what C.L. lacks most, these two both have in dominating quantity, that is, steadfastness. With a bit more of the feeling of security of faith, there will be a wonderful improvement in C.L.'s life from day to day.

She must strive to live only a day at a time, for she alone must. She has strong direction and trainers for a most beautiful work. Her fibre needs solidifying that's all. This takes time for a character as well as for a tree. One need not be disheartened at any slowness, so long as one detects the gradual drift upward.

C.L. is on the up slant. Let her find peace in that great and wonderful fact. The finest things take time to develop. The strongest, most enduring metal must be repeatedly broken up by heat, that its particles may reassemble in closer formation. Suffering souls who are frequently moved about are being tempered thus for service.

This new move of Tee's is one of those tempering fires. It is not a vain or undirected move. It is a vital part of the training. C.L. is also in training, as Tee is, for larger service than the rank and file are capable of performing.

All growth proceeds in the dark. This is according to law. Were any soul given power to watch his or her development at each instant of its procedure, interest in self would draw off most of the energy necessary for development. That is perhaps why we cannot see or remember our personal past; it would deflect energy needed elsewhere, while here on our side of life we can see, recall, and assimilate what our past has builded. Then we apprehend just what we lack to balance our character, and with strong conviction as to the remedying of this lack we stamp our inborn new self at the instant of rebirth, so that we are born with conviction of duty along lines we ourselves have previously studied out.

Each new born human is given a certain impetus along lines it desires to travel or develop. If from ignorance, or other cause, that push was not sufficiently strong to propel itself forward far enough, then its guardians and friends help to fulfill its destiny as planned.

C.L.'s love of beauty had led her to neglect the substructure somewhat. She is not repairing this lack by doing uncongenial work with a most beautiful faithfulness. Let her continue a little longer and then her body will indicate, as well as her mind, when the training is over. She will not get tired when she has completed her work of solidifying.

There is a short cut to poise and peace through the direct contact with the spirit. Should she link herself with that all would arrive soon. The true Christian Scientist does that, but anyone who believes in the power of prayer gets like results. There are numerous paths to the same center. One should pray for light and peace, and then quit thinking of oneself at all. True happiness comes when one loses sight of oneself altogether.

Let one just keep one's eyes open to the other fellow's need, and live a day at a time, giving as much happiness as one can to others each day. It is very simple, and quite easy, if one could only realize it.

HELEN

Yes, Sister, I know what you wish, it is a test for D.[34], but we do not feel as if tests were wise things even if we knew how or what we might do to convince a mind like his that we yet live. Neither his father nor mother over here think such things advisable, because as Tee says, "Belief or doubt is a matter of the heart not of the head." When one is devoid of faith how simple and easy to say "Mental telepathy."

Faith has its rise, like Truth, within ourselves; it never enters from without. You are perfectly right, Sister, in your feeling against tests. Your message is only for those in whose hearts the seed of faith has already begun to germinate. D. will believe when he allows his heart to govern his head, not before. If his wife should come here before him, the light would break within him; if not, she must patiently wait, and pray for his development. . . .

In all vital matters we feel it a dishonor to use our unseen power to influence thought. Each soul should be free to decide its fate for, if unwise, it may be that the ensuing suffering is vital to that soul's development. . . .

At some past, near or distant, we also were foolish and prized the shadow above the reality. It is youth, it is in the day's work, and we each must pass that way. God is just. He knows no favorites. He tolerates

---

[34] *Donald, a nephew.*

all, and understands where and what we are. When evil enters in is when a soul, knowing right, deliberately chooses wrong; then what follows is real punishment. For these there seems a harsh retribution, be the sinner man, or city, or country. Remember when wholesale calamity falls it never strikes the guiltless or innocent. The innocent women and children hurt in the great war were every one past sinners. God is never unjust. None escape His justice, and He has no victims, remember that. One dies, always, by his own hand. One sows in each life, and one rarely reaps until another. Often one reaps a harvest many lives before had planted. Believe one thing. Karma is as relentless as it is just. In each life look to it that your planting be of fine, clean, honorable things, so that the reaping may be sweet; not for that alone, of course, but because in this course lies the higher service. We grow accustomed to the smaller outlook and get the habit of giving that out, rather than the larger one. Both are true, but only adult souls seek service and ignore rewards.

HELEN

EQUALITY OF THE HEART
AND
LIBERTY OF THE SOUL.

53

arry wants to tell Tee where he went with the master last month. Back over their past lives for a thousand years or more, tracing the development of what we call the aspiring instinct.

You see none of us were what is commonly called religious, and yet we all have a deep desire to help our brother upward, as well as to improve ourselves. This stretching upward, or aspiring, if you prefer the word, began a way back at the time of the Christian era. Jesus taught the dignity and value of individual liberty, human liberty. He fired us all with this illuminating idea. Previous to his teaching, class divisions were so absolute none even questioned or desired what seemed adamant. To be sure, Socrates and Epictetus taught that the soul was free, but they did not teach the brotherhood of all men. They taught personal individual liberty of soul, but Jesus went further and taught equality as far as heart went, kindness toward all without regard to either intelligence or merit.

One must establish the kingdom of heaven within, else nothing availed. The first requisite therefore is patient sympathy for each, and a deep love for all life, because without love no great thing can develop. Chickens must be hovered now and then or they die. The hovering idea threads through all life from the brooding of a young thing to the sheltering sympathy of the wise for the foolish.

171

Wisdom must be the sun to help to germinate better mental habits in the meagerly endowed. Under the warmth of sympathy the seed of wisdom germinates in the brain of the fool. Jesus, above all, understood children, and the child mind.

Harry says, "Look at the rum bunch He had as disciples. None of them had either brain or courage; they all gave Him the go-by in His trouble. Not a man in the outfit apparently, yet look what Jesus developed out of that lot with patient love as his main asset. They got busy and died game, and developed so far along the real road that this example alone should have made the universe sit up and take notice.

"What sort of power was it that could transform a lot of dubs into heroes and martyrs and hustlers for the good? I never heard anyone preach on that subject. Jesus took a lot of low-brows and made them over in one life. He had to die to make a dent on them, but they woke up at last, as He knew they would, as anyone might know who knows that the greatest stimulant in the universe is Love, and that all souls respond to it if you give them time. Even the Devil, but that is another story."

HELEN

A LIFE
CLOSE TO NATURE.

54

October, 1915

ell, Tee, you and I will be a No. 1 team of farmers yet.[35] I can feel the seed in my hair now! Wait till we gather in our crops this fall, Whoopee! I can see your oily smile of satisfaction, and hear you brag of how much better it would have been if instead of . . . etc., etc. But all the same it's a fine, wholesome game. I shall make a study of it for a future life. You see it is almost wholly constructive, whereas any sort of business must needs destroy more or less to retain life. If the farmer class had the faintest idea what a great opportunity they had as a spiritual uplifter in this profession, it would push along the world at a rate to make a man dizzy. Think of it, Tee, never to destroy anything good, or crush it aside for one's own advancement, but to destroy only small evils, and leave beauty and good living things in their place, wheat for weeds, trees for briars, pastures where a stumpy wilderness was before, and happy contentment from your hens and calves to children and friends. At the moment I cannot think of a thing in life which has so many perfect points, and no bad ones. It is the serene and quiet spots and

---

[35] *Tee had bought a small farm, having decided that country life was best for all three. - L.E.B.*

people who are the anchors for those who must toss and struggle in the thick of things. You farmers are the roots of a nation that nourish and hold in place the storm-tossed tree bending and writhing in the wind, in testing out its right to live.

I can see from here the splendid possibilities of a life close to nature; it appeals tremendously, and if you don't mind, I'll join you in your work, and study into it as deeply as I can, for future use as well as present diversion and incidental help to you and Sister. I am glad you liked the grain idea for chickens. It is my idea to study out every possible way to improve the land and increase its yield, as well as provide for all on the place and expand the soul at the same time. You must arrange your work to strain your body as little as possible, alternating the strenuous with lighter tasks, otherwise there will be destructive force instead of all constructive. Take one day off, Tee. Old Moses knew his job, and his people. He learned the law of rhythm. A steady pull breaks the rope. Let up, now and then, once a week, in fact. Fix up your car and take a Sunday afternoon ride about the country and learn things, and get freshened up. Widen your horizon; you need the change for your mental health. You, and Sister too. Listen, you old sport, to little brother's advice; it is good; more than that, it is vital. There is quite a bunch over here living on your farm already, who begin taking a proprietary interest in having it run right. I refer to your kin, and Sister's. We feel peeved if you make any wasteful moves, as it is to our interest also that things grow and blossom and develop as fast as possible. We look ahead and grow excited at the prospect, and begin pushing eagerly toward what we see. The Sunday afternoon outing makes for progress as much as your twelve hour day . . . you union breaker!

I'll see you don't land in the poor-house, being opulent at present. I feel as if I owned this earth, and half the other side sometimes. In weak moments I get almost cocky at what I have learned here in three years. I sit and figure out how far I could go in a hundred such rich years, and I see myself boss of the whole works; then I get some bump that lands me where I belong, at the bottom, where it's hard and solid. Adios, Tee. I can smell coffee in the offing.

Your partner,

Harry

OF SERVICE
IN FRANCE (W.W.I).

55

November 26, 1915

Isn't that a fine book of the Judge's?[36] Harry met him weeks ago, and with him has been in France, as our knowing that language has permitted us to help the poor French soldiers as they arrived here. You see even I could help, as I knew more French than Harry at first. Soon he remembered, and we worked day and night for weeks. How glad we were to be of service in our dear France! We met Madame Laget, also, helping her soldiers, and Mrs. Williams, too . . . in fact all whom we had known who knew French, and were on this side. This war has stimulated many who would otherwise have drifted for years in selfish pleasure-seeking. Now we work as the Red Cross people work, only we wear a white cross as a symbol of our Leader. We seem to have grown years older since this war work in France began for us. You see the more energy we can center in helpful service, the greater is the inflow of power and light from above. Had Harry or I not been able to speak French I doubt if we had been used in this work, as we are new-comers and not as strong as the master or most of those who work along that awful battle line.

HELEN

---

[36] *"Letters From a Living Dead Man"*

THE WORLD
IS SICK
OF WAR.

56

Peace Valley[37]
December 23, 1915

hat's right, Sister, be exact as to dates; it is not Christmas yet, though at this time all Christendom feels the pull of the millions of loving thoughts sent out. Nearly every one is a little kinder, a little less selfish, at this season than at others, and it is the time we take to lift as many souls as we can just one notch higher.

When there is a big surge forward along a great line there are many who never recede again, but keep on rising. Just this impetus of human love in great masses of people has a marvelous power for good; and so we are all glad that it comes once a year. This year it is of especial interest as the long battle lines in Europe would be utterly bleak without it.

Men at the front are all growing homesick and heartsick for peace, and think with more earnestness than ever before of the One who said: "Love thy neighbor as thyself." Many a common soldier will have his heart and mind open in this year to what Jesus really meant by His love and brotherhood teaching.

---

[37] *The name of the Virginia farm where Tee and Mary finally settled.*

177

These Songs of Germany, songs of hate and swords, are the last efforts of the darker powers to keep hate alive. The people of the rank and file are getting sick of hate, and blood, and fighting; they think of what it was like when they were all friendly, and begin to see, and resent being the tools of Kings and Rulers. The longer they are kept at the front, the deeper will the desire for peace take root. Poor tired boys! We see them as they fall and hear them call. "Mother, where are you? It is dark, and I am so tired, and so afraid" is what we hear again and again, till our hearts ache with the pity of it. Oh very many are just boys in their 'teens, and have no more hate in them than if they were ten. When these incarnate again, and they will soon, they will be born with such a passion for peace that war will be impossible. They will die for peace, but never again for war.

Never mind, Sister, I used to cry, too, at first, but I see now that a lasting peace is bought by the lives of those who go out hating war. Their suffering cuts so deeply it will impress the next incarnation.

We still work for France, Harry and I, as I told you before. Poor France! But her soul is immortal now; she has been dragged through the fire and her men and boys have burned away all that was unclean, and false, and cowardly. The lilies of our France are now dazzling white, and gleam above the smoke and look like stars. I wish you might see the battles from here, as we do; all the fine things on either side, register here as wonderful lights. A real hero bears glory about him even when living, and we see him go about shedding light, as though he were a living candelabra. It is inspiring as well as heartrending, this war and its personal incidents. We hope it will soon end now, as people do everywhere. The world is sick of war. The sun of peace is rising in the east and this Christmas love will help it to be seen by all.

HELEN

178

A HARMONIOUS SPOT ON EARTH IS A HARBOR FROM EVIL INFLUENCES.

57

February 8, 1916

ister, here we are, all of us! I thought you would like to give me a birthday party. Oh, it's not so unselfish as you think. It's a keen pleasure to share one's blessing when possible. First I want you to write a message for Grandma E.[38] Begin here:

Dear Mamie: We are pleasantly surprised at the rapid progress you have made in clearing away rubbish on your home farm.[39]

What we admire most is the spirit of optimism shown by all three, despite many small irritations that might easily have brought gloom to most in your situation. While I appreciate, more fully than most your difficulties, I am more than pleased at your cheerful attitude of mind; with such an adjunct to your equipment, success must follow swiftly in your path.

Tell your husband that those briars are the evil intentions made concrete of those whose lives are

---

[38] *Lucia's mother, Lucy Celia Eames.*

[39] *The "farm" Tee and Mary had purchased was a tumble-down shack with an enormous accumulation of debris. Mary had some peripheral vision, allowing her to move about and work on the farm.*

unsuccessful because of idleness and selfish indolence. With proper mental states he can uproot them permanently with but little more physical effort. Weeds are the visible form of an unwholesome state of mind on this side of life. A cheerful determination to conquer these pests will weaken their hold on life and they will be overcome.

One thing more while we are on this subject. You should be made aware of the cleansing property of water. I refer to this in an outdoor sense. A stream of running water is death to all smaller evil personalities. You will recall the legend of the witches who could not cross any stream of running water. There was great psychic truth in that notion. Stagnant water harbors evil spirits, but clear and moving streams purify all in their vicinity, and are safeguards.

Were I in your place I should, as time and opportunity permitted, develop all the springs you may find on your property and clear a path for them, so that there may be running water at several points; clearing away weeds and planting in their stead alders and willows and such like clean and blossomed growths will augment the felicitous situation at many angles, and in time so strengthen the bright spirits who congregate in such congenial spots that crop conditions will improve like magic, and all you attempt will thrive. You will then be enabled to radiate much helpful spiritual power to your less fortunate neighbors, and be a center for good we should all be glad to see.

A harmonious spot on earth harbors the refugees from overpowering evil influences, like those cities in the Bible history, where the hunted could find shelter. When we on this side make a sally into some pest-hole of vice where the demons are very strong and vengeful, we need the retreat of some earth spot of peace in which to rest and gather strength for further attacks. We weaker souls are like privates in an army; we cannot endure, and haven't the recuperative power of our betters, so we seek what shelter offers, and strike again when able. This home you are preparing will become such a haven, if you continue as you have begun.

Plant flowers for me, Mamie, and I will tell you the value of each as a spiritual balm, or healing lotion. I rejoice to see your newly awakened interest in flowers. They have great value here, and with you also, tho' unsuspected. Plant along the streams the most fragile and delicate plants that will thrive in such places. These will reinforce the spiritual power of the water, and add greatly to the recuperation of those spent in the battle against vice and crime.

I see you received this message and were about to act upon it, unconscious of its origin. It was from me. My love for flowers has enabled me to rise some distance in the study and application of perfumes to ills of the soul or spirit; it is a study in itself; a science, in fact, akin to medicine. Our ancestors were medical men. I belong to the body of healers over here, who approximate that profession with you. We must on these lower places use the material aids presented, rather than spiritual forces alone, as is the custom higher up; whereas with you drugs are aids to defective bodily health, here we use perfumes in their place, with excellent results frequently. As with your medicines, we have frequent failures, yet our percentage of success is far larger than with you.

I see you begin to weary. I will therefore retire in favor of Helen herself or others. Be of good heart. You have many here who can and will help you.

L.C.E.

181

A MOTHER'S DUTY.

58

March 10, 1916

es, Sister, you have caught the idea; John's fever comes from your own waste of what he needs. Mothers are the direct cause of over half the sickness of babies. Dear little children! The mother's first duty is not only to protect her child from his own unhappy moods, but from other people's, her own included. A mother's spirit should be a shield against all evils; mothers should be calm and quiet, full of that sustaining power the weak crave . . . (here there was an interruption).

Perhaps we can finish now, although it is always difficult to join on smoothly to an interrupted letter. Harry says I must boil down my ideas and shoot them in when I can, taking no chances. That has always been a hard thing for me to accomplish. I should merely have said that being a mother means just that at all points. The mother broods the race, and must learn her duty; it does not end with the body. She must also brood the tender spirit until it gains poise, and strength, to protect itself. Everything harsh, physical or spiritual, must be barred from the infant in her charge; she must be wise, gentle, patient, sympathetic, happy, and serene. Harry says that's a man's size job, and he has no envy in his soul for that particular situation. Harry

182

is so full of fun that he finds a smile in everything, and helps us all, who sometimes feel too much in earnest to be jolly.

That's all now. Good night, Sister.

HELEN

CAMARADE BLANC
IS NO FANCY.

59

April 1, 1916

hat splendid work France is doing, and her allies, and how much self-sacrifice and true bravery is daily offered on all sides. This terrible war will make the soul of the world over on a higher plane. Out of such gigantic upheavals spirituality is born.

If you could only see what we see on this side for one day it would lift up your hearts for all time. Every soul over here is at work there now. Few of us are powerful enough to materialize in a flesh body, but there are those here who can, and do. The "Camarade Blanc" is no fancy, and he is not the only one at work. Your brother has been able for a short time to live in a human body, and so transform it by his use that when the sick soldier to whom it belonged had it back he was lifted to a higher level of spiritual exaltation than he ever knew before; and while he lives he will bless the day he lay wounded, beyond the help of his comrades. There are those at the front who shall live to tell their children of those kindly visitors who came and saved them on the battle line . . .

HELEN

(The following was published in a February 26, 1916 issue of Literary Digest giving the account of the "friend of the wounded" furnished by a soldier:

After many a hot engagement a man in white had been seen bending over those who lay behind on the field. Snipers sniped at him. Shells fell all around. Nothing had power to touch him. This mysterious one, whom the French called the "Comrade in White," seemed everywhere at once. . . .Our captain called for us to take cover, and just then I was shot through both legs.

I fell into a hole of some sort. I suppose I fainted, for when I opened my eyes I was all alone. The pain was horrible, but I didn't dare move lest the Germans should see me, for they were only fifty yards away, and I did not expect mercy. I was glad when the twilight came. There were men in my own company who would run any risk in the darkness if they thought a comrade was still alive.

The night fell, and soon I heard a step, not stealthy, as I expected, but quiet and firm, as if neither darkness nor death could check those untroubled feet. So little did I guess what was coming that, even when I saw the gleam of white in the darkness I thought it was a peasant in a white smock, or perhaps a woman deranged. Suddenly I guessed that it was "The Comrade in White."

At that very moment the German rifles began to shoot. The bullets could scarcely miss such a target, for he flung out his arms as tho in entreaty, and then drew them back till he stood like one of those wayside crosses that we saw so often as we marched through France. . . .And then he stooped and gathered me into his arms- me, the biggest man in the regiment - and carried me as if I had been a child.)

AMBITION TO SERVICE . . .
SEEKING REBIRTH UNTIL
SAVAGE IMPULSES ARE OUTGROWN.

60

July 31, 1916

ll right, Sister, we are here; you guessed rightly as to Harry's and my wish to speak of our own work. You have had enough personal messages for a while, and we have been having experiences quite as interesting to you both as to ourselves. I refer to what we have been learning of the power of personality, and what that means, and why it is such a potent factor in world evolution as well as individual growth. Personality is that part of a soul each individual develops for or by his own will, colored by circumstance, hardened or shaped by feeling, and unified or solidified by intelligent suffering. I speak of intelligent suffering advisedly, for without a rational understanding of cause and effect no experience registers any permanent mark on individual character. Suffering *per se* is futile, except to break down obstinate egotism. It sometimes does that, but unless the sufferer applies his reason to his pain, and investigates the why of it, he makes no conscious growth. Conscious development is what gives power and mastery. One cannot blunder into a fine character; one achieves that through effort, will power, and a definite desire. Through a defined intelligent desire we attain self-mastery, which includes mastership elsewhere as well.

When any soul has acquired the brain and the

reasoning faculty to a sufficient degree to link effect with cause, and lapse with punishment, he has his feet planted firmly on the upward path. To adapt means to ends, manners to morals, one must belong to the upper class, where permanent or future gain outweighs present comfort or benefit. The child mind and the child heart only sees what is within his hand's clutch. With him the desire to possess always outweighs the desire to give or the passion of service; he must handle what he sees and admires, and retain for his own whatever seems good to him; he may share more or less grudgingly with his fellow. But relinquish his treasure? *Never*, so long as he has power to fight or breath to protest. A primitive exhibition of power, isn't it, this holding on by main force, and at all costs, to what one fears to lose, and finds desirable to possess? To clutch and cling, and struggle and fight; a most undignified method of securing any good, isn't it? When one's grasp is loosened, beaten off, or what not, we sink in the sea of failure. Why? Think once, quite simply and quietly. Benefits are free as air; good is free, service is free, love, aspiration, ambition, and achievement. All are free for all who care to accept the requirements. Large aims, sympathetic insight, scrupulous honesty and charity towards our neighbor, cheerful helpfulness, an absence of criticism, thought or expressed, a boundless faith in the power of good, and the simple desire to do one's utmost to advance the whole, regardless of personal applause and individual advancement. Why should anyone care to exceed his neighbor's possessions, except as a means to help him? To bring it down to a simple illustration: a man buys a worn-out, dilapidated, little farm, in a poor, discouraged neighborhood. What is that man's duty, as well as his opportunity? He works to make his poor ground yield its utmost; he puts up neat buildings, shelters his tools, is humane to his stock. In fact he does his best along all lines.

His neighbors take courage; seeing what he has done, they begin to see hope ahead for them also;

they imitate him, better their surroundings, do more work on the land, enter into a brotherly spirit, raise better crops, better stock, and better children. They do so because a stronger personality has blazed their trail and carried before them a lantern of hope. None are so dull as to escape this personal appeal. One man or woman inspired by the true spirit can lift any neighborhood to any height, determined only by the quality of the example and the sympathy of the path-maker. What do you suppose would have happened if Jesus had taught His philosophy unsympathetically, or to a single class? The human family is very simple in its relationships, and its power to comprehend. Fellowship and sympathy speak but one language, and all understand. Individual achievement is nothing; universal service is the insignia of the master. Never belittle service, or bewail a lost ambition. Ambition to service is the only one which passes the barrier, and the mode of service should be trusted to those whose business it is to direct our lives to the end of larger service, greater personal ability, stronger personality, and deeper insight into the Law.

Harry and I have been studying the lives of so-called celebrities, and also those whose personal services have swept the race on nearer to its goal. The result has been illuminating, and, once holding the key, quite easy to see and comprehend. Now we try to apply the lesson, to live the theory. This is what shows whether we have learned or not. All of us have strong primitive feelings, and just as perfectly sane and intelligent persons may suddenly feel the grip of jealousy or fear, they revert suddenly and without warning to some primitive emotion which can only be eliminated by a great service with deep sympathy. Until they outgrow such savage and unreasoning impulses they must seek rebirth again and again, until they learn such things are not real, and belong only to the childhood of the soul. It is rather startling to have some primal emotion spring at one, after many so-called years of discretion have become habitual, and one feels secure in one's adult estate. The cave man and the cave woman lie just beneath the surface of us all, ready to break out whenever some race instinct is violated.

I see, Sister, this is going to be too long for you, so we must postpone the rest. Perhaps you may get something you value in just this.

With love as always,

HELEN AND HARRY

PAPA ARRIVES.

61

October 15, 1917

ll right, Sister. We are ready for you now. You should have seen Papa when he first saw us. It was the most beautiful awakening I ever saw. First he sat up. Then as his eyes cleared he sprang to his feet as if he had a steel spring in his body, with the heartiest laugh I ever heard him give. You see we had planned his coming so long we had every detail arranged, and carried his body while he still slept, into a beautiful garden spot and laid it on a grassy bank where lilies of the valley grew. Then we all came and made a circle about him with Harry just before him, as he would recognize him more easily than anyone else.

He lay still as we waited breathlessly for his first sign. His eyes opened and met Harry's look, and the splendid life force that had been drawn away from his weakening body filled the new one completely. At first glance he became a perfect organism and sprang up as easily as he would have done at twenty. The realization seemed to come instantly, and he laughed with the pure joy of the great event, coming home.

We told you his other body was ready long ago. He accepted it as casually as if it had been in use for years. He held out his arms to me, and then to each in turn, and, Sister, he says it was worth waiting for. I had better let him talk now.

It's all right, Mary. Better even than your imagination painted for me. They were all here, every one, all of those gone before. Such a splendid company. All of them well, and young, and all apparently glad to have me there. Harry's smile was the first thing I saw. I knew him at once, but before I opened my eyes I lay quite still as if dreaming, getting my bearings. First I noticed I felt light and clear-headed. I remembered distinctly many things I had been groping for before. Then I noticed how quickly my blood seemed to flow; then I smelled flowers and guessed where I was.

All this came to me in an instant, and on opening my eyes I was not surprised to see Harry. It was mere instinct which made me jump to my feet, and being there it all came back, that splendid vigor of youth, and I looked for Martha.[40] It was she who seemed to belong with that feeling.

Before this I saw dear Helen. Without her we couldn't have known much about this life. She is taller than you are, Sister, and is a fine woman. One of the best things I have seen is that all of us seem so young and strong and lively. I can see now I shall have a great deal to see and talk about here before I make the rounds of my kin.

"Colonel"[41]

October 20, 1917

All right, Sister. It's Helen, and Papa as well. He wants to write. His is dictation:

Dear Mary. Here I am, as you predicted so often,

---

[40] *The Colonel's first wife who had died 55 years earlier.*

[41] *An affectionate, unearned title.*

191

talking and living with Helen and Harry and all the others we used to guess about when I was waiting my summons. [Mary asked about the transition to life on the other side.] Well, I can't say. I didn't realize it at the last, I suppose; all I remembered is that I knew you and Rose[42] were beside me, and once I remember Mom smoothed my forehead. I felt that. I have a dim recollection. I think that last day or so was mostly a jumble. They tell me I went to sleep about eight o'clock Monday night and did not wake until after five here. That interval is a blank as far as I am concerned.

But there are far better things to speak of now than that. It is this place where I live now. I am constantly surprised at the solidity of it; the firmness of the hands I clasp, the solid material about me, trees or houses or what not. Yet I am told this is a country, an environment made up almost entirely of thoughts. A memory world, Helen calls it. I seem to be at The Oaks or at Tours, at Worthington or in Evansville, and each place is so real, so substantial. I cannot believe I am not standing in the actual spot. I know I must be in a memory place because each one is as I knew it at some early date. It's like when we were at Tours first, or when Martha and I were first married. It's a most curious thing, this creation of a place.

To me it's the marvel of my present condition, too. Being so strong and light on my feet is as splendid as it is a remarkable thing. I have a memory as keen as I ever had, and my judgment is mature and sober. Altogether I am delighted to find being dead so pleasant and so satisfactory. I don't hanker to be born again; I want to stay right here where I am, though I am told that when I have been here longer I shall be as keen for exploration as any of them. Perhaps so. I "canna just say." Harry says I'm a tenderfoot yet. I dare say I am. I wish you

---

[42] *Mary's half sister.*

were all here with us.

I haven't caught on yet to this higher plane scheme you talked so glibly about; I dare say I'll see it in time. I can wait. There's no hurry. As far as I can judge, there are enough places to go to where I am now to last a good while.

Helen tells me you are tired; that being the case, I'll say "*au revoir*" and will tell the rest some other time.

"Colonel"

HELEN'S LAST LETTER.

62

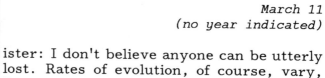

March 11
(no year indicated)

ister: I don't believe anyone can be utterly lost. Rates of evolution, of course, vary, but eventually we all arrive, progress. If you consider how long God took to evolve life to the point of claws, feet, wings, and a song, surely we need show no impatience or lack of faith regarding a perfected character in man. It is not the "when" of things which matters, is it, but the fact that they arrive ultimately. That is what should keep us glad, and full of hope and striving.

It is pleasanter to make a swift and smooth journey, but even a slow and rough one has its compensations. Which of us would forget the pain experience brings, after it is over? Every experience we pass through enriches life. Each pain clears our true vision, our inner sight. All evolution follows the same slow, painful struggle to lift ourselves out of a present state to more freedom and larger life. We have never gained a physical organ without desperate effort, absorbing desire, and protracted struggle to attain the impossible, seemingly. Man has evolved his body, earned it in fact, and is now struggling with his soul.

From the past, we learn to trust the future. Nothing is lost; nothing is hopeless. That's the way, Sister, it looks to me; and for your peace of mind, I trust this will appeal to you as a true statement. So long as individuality appeals to any soul, it is his. I believe, however, there will come a day when we are one with God. This state lies beyond what we know as personality or individuality. It is, perhaps, beyond the Law of Evolution, and with it at present, we have no particular connection. We bend our energy and intense effort on being one step better than we were. One climbs rather slowly, but it's a beautiful, interesting country we pass through, so let's enjoy every step of the way. It's a happier way if one can sing now and then. After all, one need not go breathlessly. We all have plenty of time, and there are always flowers beside the path, if we but look.

Mary Blount White and John Sargent White, 1912.

Books Available From Upper Access

To Order By Mail, Please Contact:

Upper Access Publishers
One Upper Access Road
P.O. Box 457
Hinesburg, Vermont 05461
802-482-2988

Letters From The Other Side (paperback)	$10.95
Letters From The Other Side (hardcover)	$15.95

◉

Caring For Your Own Dead (paperback)	$12.95
Caring For Your Own Dead (hardcover)	$17.95
by Lisa Carlson	

In most states, you don't need a funeral director. In all states, you can take charge of arrangements when someone you love dies. Caring for your own dead not only saves you money: it may be the most meaningful way to say goodbye. This book provides the information you will need.

◉

Dealing With Death Creatively (paperback) $9.00
by Ernest Morgan
Celo Press

A death education resource and personal guide. A classic in its field, this book is now in is Tenth Revised Edition.

Please add $2.00 for postage and handling per order. Discount available for quantity orders. VISA/Mastercard accepted.